FRANCE
THE VEGETARIAN TABLE

FRANCE
THE VEGETARIAN TABLE

BY GEORGEANNE BRENNAN

PHOTOGRAPHY BY JOHN VAUGHAN

PHOTO STYLING BY JODY THOMPSON-KENNEDY

FOOD STYLING BY KAREN FRERICHS

CHRONICLE BOOKS · SAN FRANCISCO

Props provided by La Bouquetiere, Ashling, Chez Mac, RH, Pierre Deux, and Sue Fisher King
in San Francisco; Hastings & Hastings and Summerhouse in Mill Valley; Nicole's Pottery
in Sonoma; and The Booneville Hotel in Booneville, California.

Library of Congress Cataloging in Publication Data available.

ISBN 0-8118-0474-7

Editing: Sharon Silva
Book Design: Louise Fili Ltd.
Design Assistant: Mahsa Safavi
Photo Styling: Jody Thompson Kennedy

Printed in Hong Kong.

Distributed in Canada by Raincoast Books,
8680 Cambie St., Vancouver, B.C. V6P 6M9

10 9 8 7 6 5 4 3 2 1

Chronicle Books
275 Fifth Street
San Francisco, CA 94103

DEDICATION

To my children, Ethel, Oliver, Tom, and Dan, and their many friends, especially Robert Wallace, who have been enthusiastic samplers and critics of all the vegetable dishes in this book. Thank you. It was fun.

GEORGEANNE BRENNAN

To Maria Miranda Gresham, who makes it all possible.

JOHN VAUGHAN

TABLE OF CONTENTS

✦

ACKNOWLEDGMENTS

MY DEEPEST THANKS TO MY FRIENDS, NEIGHBORS, COLLEAGUES, AND ACQUAINTANCES IN FRANCE WHO OVER THE LAST TWENTY-FIVE YEARS HAVE SHARED WITH ME THEIR LOVE OF FOOD AND THE PROCESS OF GROWING AND PREPARING IT. A special thank you to Hubert Keller, of the *Fleur de Lys* restaurant in San Francisco, who so graciously discussed with me his notion of French vegetarian cuisine and perused the proposed recipes when this book was still in the developmental stage; to Michael Bauer, Marianne Mariner, and Fran Irwin of the Food Section of the San Francisco Chronicle newspaper whose enthusiasms and encouragements are a perpetual source of pleasure for me; to my editors at Chronicle Books, Bill LeBlond and Leslie Jonath, for asking me to do this book and seeing it through to fruition. A special thank you to Jim Schrupp and Sharon Silva whose artful editing makes a manuscript become a book. To Ethel Brennan, thank you for the thoughtful assistance and keen eye you brought to teaching classes and to recipe testing for this book. Thank you, Susan Lescher, agent *extraordinaire.*

The photography took place under the sure and creative hands of stylist Jody Thompson-Kennedy and cooking stylist Karen Frerichs, who infused every session with not only their intense professionalism but with their ebullient enthusiasm and wonderful sense of humor. They made each working day a joyful experience. Thank you Jody and Karen! Thanks as always to the irreplaceable Maria Gresham.

FRANCE
THE VEGETARIAN TABLE

INTRODUCTION

❉

I N FRENCH COOKING, FLAVOR IS TREASURED ABOVE ALL, AND FLAVOR IS PREDICATED UPON INGREDI-ENTS THAT ARE FRESH, SEASONAL, AND REGIONAL. Vegetables are as significant in this culinary triumvirate as oysters or salmon, lamb or pheasant.

In a French kitchen, a ragout made from the garden's first tender spring vegetables elicits swoons of delight, and day after day the table will be set with early asparagus, *salades sauvages*, and earthy new potatoes. Late spring celebrates the garden's artichokes and fava beans with *tians* replete with cream or olive oil. Come summer, the peas, turnips, and carrots of spring's ragouts are forgotten and their place is taken by locally grown tomatoes, squash, eggplants, and beans served up in *soupe au pistou*, *ratatouille*, and salads of every kind. As summer wanes, wild mushrooms freshly gathered from the forest floor, sautéed with herbs, and folded into a simple *brouillade* of eggs celebrates the season, to be replaced in winter by lusty cabbage soups and winter grills of *trevise*, *courge*, and onions.

To cook *la bonne cuisine du terroir* is to use the foods of the region. Often the most intense and pleasurable flavors are those derived from what is immediate, from what is on hand in the earth. In any given region, the personal kitchen gardens and orchards—the *potagers* and *vergers*—supply seasonal vegetables and fruits that are as fresh as the length of the garden path. Fields, hillsides, meadows, forests, and streams deliver the wild greens, herbs, berries, mushrooms, game, and fish that further give food the characteristic tastes of the region. Local open-air markets, like the gardens and the *marchés*, have an individuality that reflects their *terroir*, and thus a market in Normandy will be quite different from one in Provence or in the Loire.

Although France does not have a vegetarian tradition, cooking without meat is often the case in a French kitchen. This is not because of a rejection of meat, but because of the ongoing celebration of the flavors of seasonal vegetables— of vegetables that honor the tradition of *la cuisine du terrior*. Composing menus that are both French and vegetarian presents little difficulty, since a number of classic French dishes—flans, quiches, stews, soups, gratins, *tians*, grills—rely solely on vegetables. Numerous other dishes, such as *cassoulets* and *pot au feus*, can be adapted to a meatless form. Most importantly, the fundamental premise of *la cuisine du terroir* invites interpretation and experimentation.

I have always been surprised by the intensity of the French attachment to the land and what it produces. When my husband and I had a small *troupeau* of goats in Provence, and we made and sold goat cheese, we discovered that we were a local attraction. People drove from Toulon and Hyères and from neighboring villages to buy the soft, newly made fresh cheeses directly from the farm. Our production was a regional specialty. They brought their elderly parents and their young children to see the goats, and often they showed up early in the morning or in late afternoon to watch me milk them! They also visited my neighbors, market gardeners, to buy *Charentais* melons, white peaches, or asparagus, depending upon the season. Laden with *cajots*, or wooden crates, of fresh fruits and vegetables and paper-wrapped cheeses, they happily headed back to the city, waving good-bye after a successful day in the country.

Over the years, I have come to understand that a trip to the countryside to visit friends or relatives for a Sunday lunch will be a feast of whatever is in season, and that invariably there will be an after-lunch walk to the garden or the orchard to admire and perhaps to sample what is growing. Exchanges about the size of the artichokes in comparison with the same time last year, and taste-tests between the *bigarre* cherries and the *Montmorency* are made amidst much discussion. In northern France, apples are cut into slices, passed around, and critiqued; in the south of France, the same is done with melons. Depending upon the season and the region, the after-lunch excursion might include a foray along the roadside, or into meadowlands or forests, to gather wild salad greens or garlic, *fraises des bois*, wild cherries, or mushrooms. The connection with the land is not only intense, it is personal and important, part of the *patrimonie*.

The passion for the land and what it produces is evident at the open markets, too. Intelligent discourses, not simply sales pitches, are given by vendors to their inquiring customers, and thoughtful discussions are carried on between buyer and seller about the virtues of a particular variety, the degree of ripeness, its condition of harvest and handling. It is not surprising to see a dozen vendors, all selling tomatoes, *courgettes*, peaches, and *mesclun*, and a long line at only one vendor while the others have but two or three customers. The determining factors that will cause a shopper to wait to buy the vegetables that are also available only a few paces away without waiting are quality and flavor. The French cook cares as much about the quality of a particular vegetable as about that of a cheese or a chicken. The cook's interest further extends not only to a particular vegetable in season, but to its culinary qualities at different progressions in its season. A tender, young spring turnip may be simply steamed and tossed with a little butter, while a sturdy winter turnip is given a treatment of oven-simmering in cream and herbs and a crusty topping of buttered bread crumbs. Large, starchy late-season peas or fava beans will be cooked into soup and puréed, but tiny new peas and *fèvettes* will be savored on their own with a few clippings of mint or chervil.

Provenance: du Pays posted on the black slate board that announces price and variety signals that the fruit or vegetable is locally grown. *Provenance: Espagne, Provenance: Maroc*, and *Provenance: Haute Provence* are all labels that inform the shopper. In the *marché*, the woman selling tomatoes *du pays* is likely to display her wares with a length of tomato vine attached, to let the shoppers know that the slightly irregular, green-shouldered fruits are truly local, garden-grown, vine-ripened tomatoes. The herbs sold alongside them are not only *du pays*, but are typical of the regional ingredients. Basil seedlings ready for transplanting or a branch of fresh bay laurel will distinguish a Provençal display, while further north, lush tarragon or crispy watercress would be more typical.

Other wares show the same regional differences. The cheeses *du pays* will have a distinct flavor from one region to another. In the north, the cows or goats will have been fed on lush green pastures, while those of the south will have eaten scrubby juniper, wild thyme, and oaks. Regional basics and seasonings vary, too. In the north, butter is heavily used, so in the *marchés* of Normandy and Alsace-Lorraine, blocks of locally made *beurre* are sold, but in the south these are replaced by bottles of that region's greenish gold olive oil.

The French concept of *cuisine du terroir* readily adapts to environments outside its native land. In California we find French cooks using such ethnically diverse local ingredients as cilantro and fresh water chestnuts in lieu of the sorrel and salsify of the Auvergne; in New Mexico, blue corn and *crema* replace the buckwheat crêpes and *crème fraîche* of the alps, and in the Caribbean, a delicate flan of sweet potato is served with a fruit *coulis*.

In organizing this book and presenting the recipes, I have drawn primarily upon the foods and presentations of home-style French cooking that I have learned—and continue to learn—from my French neighbors and friends. In the introduction to many of the recipes, I have given suggestions for using different vegetables, according to season, to reflect not simply the food but also the spirit of French vegetable cooking. Additionally, I have tried to choose those recipes that would most successfully lend themselves as components to the creation of meatless, yet substantial and attractive, meals that rival the meat-based repasts most Americans regularly consume.

To encourage and to allow flexibility within recipes and to further the experimentation and creativity that surrounds the French vegetarian table, the first part of the book, which is entitled "Basics," presents recipes for broths, sauces, and infusions. Many of these are used in various dishes throughout the book, plus I have included suggestions for other uses beyond these pages.

Since French meals are traditionally taken in courses, a chapter devoted to beginning plates follows. These range from light salads and soups to *beignets*, flans, and other heartier fare. Most often these recipes emphasize a single vegetable, and only occasionally a group of vegetables. I have sometimes offered ideas on which main course and dessert might follow these openers to give an idea of a pleasing menu.

Main dishes tend to be slightly more complex in flavor, and include hearty soups, ragouts, and *grillades*, among them dishes that include several different vegetables. Suggestions are made here, too, for first courses and desserts to complete a menu.

And, finally, there is a small chapter of desserts. It may seem odd to have such a section in a book about vegetables, but the inclusion of compotes, *clafoutis*, and several other home-style fruit desserts rounds out the reliance on the ebb and flow of the seasons to define and order the French table.

CHAPTER ONE

BASICS

BASICS

✳

REPERTOIRE OF VEGETABLE-BASED BROTHS, SAUCES, AND INFUSIONS READILY ALLOWS THE COOK TO VARY OR ENHANCE THE RECIPES IN THIS BOOK. These are not, for the most part, the elements of *haute cuisine* or even of a classic French kitchen. They instead belong to the simple inventory of a French home cook, even a busy one.

I have often seen Pascal, one of my neighbors in Provence, come home after a long, dusty day of masonry work and, upon first offering me an aperítif, disappear into the kitchen, only to emerge fifteen minutes later carrying a lush tomato salad liberally dressed with a homemade shallot vinaigrette. He follows the tomatoes with a platter of boiled summer vegetables and hard-cooked eggs accompanied with a bowl of freshly made *aïoli*.

One evening, walking unexpectedly into Victorine Frenet's mountain house, high above Moustiers Ste.-Marie in the Alpes-de-Haute-Provence, I had one of the best meals of my life. As we chatted, she quickly whipped up a *tapenade* of black olives and spread it on toasts grilled in the open fire. Her larder yielded up some mushrooms fresh from the neighboring pine forest, and she turned them into a delicate gratin with a light coating of parslied *béchamel* sauce. A *salade verte* dressed with her homemade black pepper–infused olive oil and wild berry vinegar was set alongside.

Tapenade to spread on croutons or serve with roasted garlic, *harissa* for couscous, creamy *béchamel*, summertime tomato *coulis*, infused oils and vinegars are all *sous les mains* of the home cook. Broths, made perhaps the night before or even a day or so in advance of their use, are quickly assembled with vegetables and herbs and left to simmer. Their aromatic essence will form the basis of soups and stews. It is an easy repertoire, yet one that personalizes and gives much fresh flavor to whatever you cook.

BROTHS

❀

BROTHS ARE EXTREMELY IMPORTANT TO ALL KINDS OF COOKING BECAUSE THEY BRING WITH THEM THE ESSENCE OF A NUMBER OF DIFFERENT INGREDIENTS—IN THIS CASE, VEGETABLES AND HERBS—REDUCED TO A PLEASING WHOLE. THE RESULT OF THIS REDUCTION IS AN INDEFINABLE RICHNESS THAT WE IDENTIFY AS FLAVOR. ❀ A VARIETY OF INGREDIENTS MAY BE USED TO MAKE VEGETABLE BROTHS, AMONG THEM THE SKINS, RINDS, SEEDS, AND STEMS OF VEGETABLES AND HERBS; DRY SPICES; AND SOMETIMES FRUITS. THESE ARE SIMMERED IN WATER, IN WATER AND WINE, OR IN OTHER LIQUID, OFTEN WITH A LITTLE BUTTER OR OIL. I DO ENCOURAGE YOU TO EXPERIMENT WITH CREATING YOUR OWN BROTHS, AS EACH SEASON AND LOCALITY IS CHARACTERIZED BY DIFFERENT FLAVORS THAT CAN BE CAPTURED IN THE STOCKPOT. ❀ I HAVE INCLUDED THREE SIMPLE VEGETABLE BROTHS THAT ARE READILY MADE AND THAT STORE WELL. THEY CAN BE KEPT IN THE FREEZER FOR UP TO SIX MONTHS OR IN THE REFRIGERATOR FOR FOUR OR FIVE DAYS.

LEEK AND MUSHROOM BROTH

MAKES 1½ TO 2 QUARTS

THIS IS MY FAVORITE ALL-PURPOSE VEGETABLE BROTH. IT HAS A RICH, SUBSTANTIAL, NONDOMINATING FLAVOR THAT MAKES A WONDERFUL POACHING LIQUID AND ENHANCES ANY DISH IN WHICH IT IS USED, WHETHER A SOUP, A SAUCE, OR A STEW.

½ pound fresh cultivated white or
    brown mushrooms, or ¼ pound each
    cultivated mushrooms and shiitake,
    chanterelle, or oyster mushrooms
4 carrots, cut into 2-inch lengths
2 large leeks, cut into 2-inch lengths
2 yellow onions, quartered
1 large celery stalk, cut into
    2-inch lengths
5 whole cloves
2 quarts water
1 teaspoon salt

Coarsely chop the mushrooms. Combine all the ingredients in a medium-sized soup pot or stockpot. Bring to a boil over medium-high heat. Cover, reduce the heat to low, and simmer until the vegetables have imparted their flavor to the broth, 45 minutes to 1 hour.

Remove from the heat and strain the broth through a fine-mesh sieve into a clean container with a tight-fitting lid. Discard the contents of the sieve. Cover the broth and refrigerate or freeze.

WINTER ROOTS AND GREENS BROTH

THE PARSNIPS GIVE THIS BROTH ITS HINT OF SWEETNESS. THE STURDY GREEN CHARD, THE PARSLEY, AND THE ROBUST CELERY BALANCE THE TASTE. THIS BROTH COMPLEMENTS VEGETABLES SUCH AS DRIED BEANS, WINTER SQUASH, KALE, CABBAGE, AND OTHER BRASSICAS.

In a large, heavy-bottomed soup pot over medium heat, warm the oil. Add the parsnips, turnip, celery, carrots, onions, chard, and parsley and sauté until the onions are translucent, 3 or 4 minutes. Add the water, star anise, salt, peppercorns, and bay leaves. Bring to a boil over medium-high heat, reduce the heat to low, and simmer, uncovered, until the vegetables and seasonings impart their flavors to the broth, about 1 hour.

Remove from the heat and strain the broth through a fine-mesh sieve into a clean container with a tight-fitting lid. Discard the contents of the sieve. Cover the broth and refrigerate or freeze.

2 tablespoons light cooking oil, such as canola

4 parsnips, cut into thick slices

1 turnip, quartered

5 celery stalks with leaves intact, cut into 2-inch lengths

4 carrots, cut into 2-inch lengths

2 yellow onions, quartered

10 large green chard leaves, coarsely chopped

2 cups chopped fresh parsley, preferably flat-leaf

2 quarts water

2 star anise

1 teaspoon salt

6 whole black peppercorns, bruised

2 fresh or dried bay leaves

BASIC VEGETABLE BROTH

VARY THE VEGETABLES ACCORDING TO THE SEASON, AND TO YOUR TASTE. CARROTS, CELERY, PARSLEY, LEEKS, AND ONIONS ENSURE AN ESSENTIAL FLAVOR BASE, HOWEVER.

2 tablespoons butter

6 large carrots, cut into 2-inch lengths

1 head celery, stalks separated and cut
    into 2-inch lengths

1 large celery root, peeled and cut into
    4 or 5 large pieces

2 large leeks, cut into 2-inch lengths

1 bunch parsley (about 1 cup), preferably
    flat-leaf, coarsely chopped

1 bunch chervil (about ½ cup),
    coarsely chopped

2 yellow onions, quartered

½ pound English peas in their pods

2 fresh or dried bay leaves

2 quarts water

1½ teaspoons salt

8 whole black peppercorns

In a large, heavy-bottomed soup pot over medium heat, melt the butter. When it begins to foam, add the carrots, celery, celery root, leeks, parsley, chervil, onions, peas, and bay leaves and cook, turning often, for 4 or 5 minutes. Add the water, salt, and peppercorns and bring to a boil over medium-high heat. Reduce the heat to low, cover, and simmer for about 45 minutes. Uncover and simmer for another 45 minutes until the vegetables and seasonings impart their flavors to the broth. Taste for salt, adding more if desired.

Remove from the heat and strain the broth through a fine-mesh sieve into a clean container with a tight-fitting lid. Discard the contents of the sieve. Cover the broth and refrigerate or freeze.

VINAIGRETTES

✷

VINAIGRETTES ARE THE PRINCIPAL SALAD DRESSINGS OF FRANCE. THEY ARE USED FOR GREEN SALADS OF ALL KINDS AND TO DRESS STEAMED OR GRILLED VEGETABLES AND RICE OR OTHER GRAIN-BASED SALADS. TRADITIONALLY, VINAIGRETTES ARE MIXTURES OF OIL AND VINEGAR, ALTHOUGH SOMETIMES LEMON OR ANOTHER ACIDIC JUICE IS USED IN PLACE OF THE VINEGAR. THE MIXTURES ARE COMMONLY SEASONED WITH SALT AND PEPPER, BUT SHALLOTS, ONIONS, OR GARLIC MIGHT BE ADDED, OR PERHAPS SHARP MUSTARD OR MINCED HERBS. ◉ OLIVE OIL IS USED THROUGHOUT FRANCE FOR VINAI-GRETTES, EVEN THOUGH IT IS INDIGENOUS ONLY TO THE MEDITERRANEAN REGION OF THE COUNTRY. A FIRST COLD-PRESSED OLIVE OIL IS BEST, AS IT HAS THE TRUEST FLAVOR. RED WINE VINEGAR IS THE MOST FREQUENTLY USED VINEGAR, ALTHOUGH WHITE IS USED AS WELL, AND, IN THE APPLE-PRODUCING REGIONS, CIDER VINEGAR IS OFTEN PREFERRED. RATIOS OF OIL TO VINEGAR WILL VARY DEPENDING UPON THE FLAVOR AND STRENGTH OF THE VINEGAR AND THE TASTE AND QUALITY OF THE OLIVE OIL. CONSIDER A RATIO OF ONE-THIRD VINEGAR TO TWO-THIRDS OLIVE OIL, UNLESS YOU HAVE A TRULY GLORIOUS OIL, IN WHICH CASE, ONE-FOURTH VINEGAR TO THREE-FOURTHS OLIVE OIL IS DESIRABLE. ◉ VINAIGRETTES MAY BE STORED REFRIGERATED FOR TEN TO FOURTEEN DAYS. BRING THEM TO ROOM TEMPERATURE BEFORE USING.

CLASSIC VINAIGRETTE

MAKES 1 CUP

WHEN I HAVE A VERY GOOD OLIVE OIL ON HAND—RICH, FULL-BODIED, FRUITY—THIS IS THE ULTI-MATE SALAD DRESSING. AFTERWARDS, I WILL TAKE A BIT OF BREAD AND SOAK UP ANY POOLS OR DROPS LEFT GLISTENING ON MY PLATE, AND ENCOURAGE EVERYONE ELSE TO DO THE SAME. ◉ ON A SALAD OF YOUNG, TENDER LETTUCE, THOUGH, USE THIS VINAIGRETTE SPARINGLY, MIXING IT IN GENTLY WITH YOUR HANDS SO AS NOT TO BRUISE THE GREENS. HEAVIER APPLICATIONS, AS WELL AS THE STRONGER VERSIONS THAT CALL FOR GARLIC AND MUSTARD, COMPLEMENT ASSERTIVE FLAVORS, SUCH AS THE WILD GREENS OF A **SALADE SAUVAGE**, A HEARTY ROMAINE, ROASTED SWEET PEPPERS, OR BOILED BEETS.

¾ cup first cold-pressed olive oil
½ teaspoon salt
½ teaspoon freshly cracked black pepper
¼ cup red wine vinegar

In a bowl, whisk together the olive oil, salt, and pepper until the olive oil thickens and changes color slightly. Whisk in the vinegar until it is well incorporated.

SHALLOT VINAIGRETTE: Add 2 to 3 tablespoons minced shallots to Classic Vinaigrette, whisking them in along with the salt and pepper.

GARLIC VINAIGRETTE: Add 1 clove garlic, minced, to Classic Vinaigrette, whisking it in along with the salt and pepper.

MUSTARD VINAIGRETTE: Add 1 tablespoon Dijon-style mustard to Classic Vinaigrette, whisking it in with the salt and pepper.

GARLIC AND MUSTARD VINAIGRETTE: Add 1 clove garlic, minced, and 1 tablespoon Dijon-style mustard to Classic Vinaigrette, whisking them in with the salt and pepper.

TARRAGON VINAIGRETTE

MAKES 1 CUP

USE THIS FRAGRANT VINAIGRETTE TO DRESS GRATED CARROTS, BOILED NEW POTATOES, STEAMED ASPARAGUS, OR EARLY SUMMER SQUASH. IT IS ALSO A GOOD CHOICE FOR SALADS THAT INCLUDE CITRUS OR MINT.

In a bowl, whisk together the olive oil, salt, pepper, and shallots until the olive oil thickens and changes color slightly. Whisk in the vinegar until it is well incorporated, then stir in the minced tarragon, if using.

½ cup first cold-pressed olive oil

½ teaspoon salt

½ freshly ground or cracked black pepper

1 tablespoon minced shallots

⅓ cup tarragon vinegar, homemade (see page 39) or purchased

1 tablespoon minced fresh tarragon (optional)

VINAIGRETTE OF LEMON JUICE WITH PARSLEY

MAKES ABOUT 1 CUP

THIS VINAIGRETTE SHOULD TASTE LEMONY, BUT NOT MAKE YOUR MOUTH PUCKER. IT IS EXCELLENT ON SALADS MADE OF GREENS FROM THE CHICORY FAMILY, ESPECIALLY RADICCHIO. IT ALSO PARTNERS WELL WITH STEAMED OR BOILED POTATOES, COOKED WHITE BEANS OR LENTILS, GREEN SNAP BEANS OR ARTICHOKES.

In a bowl, whisk together the olive oil, salt, pepper, and parsley until the olive oil thickens and changes color slightly. Whisk in the lemon juice until it is well incorporated.

¾ cup cold-pressed olive oil or Lemon-Infused Olive Oil (page 38)

½ teaspoon salt

1 teaspoon freshly cracked or ground black pepper

¼ cup minced fresh parsley

¼ to ⅓ cup fresh lemon juice

DOUBLE-BLACK PEPPER VINAIGRETTE

MAKES I CUP

THE FLAVOR OF SWEET PEPPERS OR SPICY GREENS SUCH AS WATERCRESS AND ARUGULA IS HEIGHT-ENED BY THIS VINAIGRETTE. IT ALSO PAIRS WELL WITH THE SLIGHTLY SOUR TASTE OF CERTAIN CHEESES, SUCH AS FETA.

¾ cup Black Pepper–Infused Olive Oil
　(page 38)
½ teaspoon salt
½ teaspoon freshly cracked or ground
　black pepper
2 tablespoons minced shallots
¼ cup red wine vinegar or Nasturtium
　Blossom Vinegar (page 41)
1 teaspoon minced fresh marjoram
　or oregano

In a small bowl, whisk together the pepper-infused olive oil, salt, pepper, and shallots until the olive oil thickens and changes color slightly. Whisk in the vinegar and marjoram until they are well incorporated.

BALSAMIC VINAIGRETTE

MAKES ABOUT I CUP

THE BEST BALSAMIC VINEGAR IS AGED IN VARIOUS WOODS, FOR AS LONG AS TWENTY YEARS, AND IT IS QUITE COMPLEX AND EVEN SWEET. THIS VINAIGRETTE GOES WELL WITH GRILLED OR ROASTED VEGETABLES, SUCH AS ONIONS AND WINTER SQUASH. IT ALSO COMPLEMENTS FRUIT SALADS AND COMPOTES.

½ cup cold-pressed olive oil
½ teaspoon salt
½ teaspoon freshly cracked black pepper
3 tablespoons minced shallots
⅓ to ½ cup balsamic vinegar

In a small bowl, whisk together the olive oil, salt, pepper, and shallots until the olive oil thickens and changes color slightly. Whisk in the vinegar until it is well incorporated.

SAUCES

✵

DESCRIBED IN THEIR SIMPLEST TERMS, SAUCES ARE THICKENED LIQUIDS THAT LEND FLAVOR TO AN ENORMOUS RANGE OF FOODS. FRENCH COOKS HAVE LONG BEEN THE RECOGNIZED MASTERS OF SAUCES, BUT SINCE MANY OF THE CLASSICS ARE RICH WITH BUTTER AND CREAM, OR ARE PRIMARILY USED TO ACCOMPANY MEAT AND FISH, I HAVE NOT INCLUDED THEM. RATHER, I HAVE EMPHASIZED VINAI-GRETTES FOR USING WITH VEGETABLES, AND SAUCES BASED ON VEGETABLES, SUCH AS **SAUCE ROUGE**, **SAUCE VERTE**, AND **COULIS DE TOMATES**. THE EXCEPTION IS **BÉCHAMEL**, THE FRENCH WHITE SAUCE THAT CAN BE USED IN A MYRIAD OF WAYS WITH COOKED VEGETABLES.

AÏOLI

MAKES ABOUT 1 CUP

MOST COOKS DESCRIBE **AÏOLI** AS SIMPLY GARLIC MAYONNAISE. IN ITS MOST SUBLIME RENDITION, IT IS RICH OLIVE OIL, EGG YOLKS, AND CRUSHED GARLIC CLOVES WHISKED TOGETHER INTO THICK SWIRLS. CLASSICALLY IT MUST BE MADE WITH A MORTAR AND PESTLE, BUT A FORK AND A BOWL WILL WORK AS WELL. YOU CAN ALSO USE A BLENDER OR SMALL FOOD PROCESSOR, ADDING THE OIL DROP BY DROP AND THEN IN A FINE, STEADY STREAM WHILE THE MOTOR IS ENGAGED. THE LONGER THE SAUCE STANDS, THE MORE INTENSE THE GARLIC FLAVOR BECOMES. THE SAUCE CAN BE STORED IN A TIGHTLY COVERED CONTAINER IN THE REFRIGERATOR FOR A FEW DAYS.

3 cloves garlic
½ teaspoon salt
2 egg yolks
1 cup olive oil

In a mortar or bowl, and using a pestle or a fork, crush and blend the garlic cloves with the salt until they are thoroughly combined. Set aside.

In a separate bowl, using a whisk, beat the egg yolks until the color changes to pale yellow, about 5 minutes.

Add the olive oil a drop at a time to the yolks, continuing to whisk until the mixture begins to thicken. Do not add the oil too quickly or the mixture will not thicken. Once it has thickened, add the remaining olive oil in a very thin but steady stream, continuing to whisk, until the desired consistency is achieved. Stir in the garlic mixture.

QUICK *AÏOLI*: In a blender or in a food processor fitted with the metal blade, combine 2 cloves garlic and 1 tablespoon olive oil. Purée until smooth. Add ¾ cup commercial mayonnaise and process until just blended. Add salt, if desired. Makes about ¾ cup.

DRIED-TOMATO *AÏOLI*: Fold ¼ cup minced, drained oil-packed dried tomatoes and ½ teaspoon of the oil in which the tomatoes were packed into ¾ cup *AÏOLI* or Quick *AÏOLI* (preceding). Makes about 1 cup.

ROASTED RED PEPPER *AÏOLI*: Roast and peel ½ sweet red pepper (page 31), then purée in a blender or small food processor fitted with the metal blade. Fold the puréed pepper into ¾ cup *Aïoli* or Quick *Aïoli* (preceding). Makes about 1 cup.

BÉCHAMEL SAUCE

MAKES ABOUT 1 CUP

BÉCHAMEL IS ONE OF THE GREAT, ALL-PURPOSE SAUCES OF CLASSIC FRENCH COOKING. I FIND IT INDISPENSABLE FOR GRATINS, ONE OF THE FINEST, SIMPLEST WAYS TO SERVE VEGETABLES. USE IT ALSO FOR NAPPING PASTA AND CRÊPE DISHES BEFORE THEY GO INTO THE OVEN AND FOR BINDING INGREDIENTS TOGETHER FOR STUFFINGS.

Melt the butter in a heavy-bottomed saucepan over medium heat. When it begins to foam, remove the pan from the heat and whisk in the flour, salt, nutmeg, and cayenne pepper until a paste forms. Return the pan to medium heat and add the milk in a slow, steady stream, whisking constantly. Reduce the heat to low and stir until no lumps remain.

Simmer the sauce, stirring occasionally, until it is thick enough to coat the back of a spoon, about 10 minutes. Taste for seasoning and adjust if necessary.

CHEESE SAUCE: Add ½ cup grated cheese, such as Gruyère or Cantal, to the finished sauce. Stir over low heat just until the cheese melts, 2 to 3 minutes. Makes about 1 cup.

2 tablespoons butter

3 tablespoons all-purpose flour

½ teaspoon salt

¼ teaspoon freshly grated nutmeg

⅛ teaspoon cayenne pepper

1 cup milk

SAUCE VERTE

MAKES ABOUT ½ CUP

MADE WITH BASIL, **SAUCE VERTE** IS, LIKE **SAUCE ROUGE**, A SUMMER SAUCE. HERE, TOO, THE THICK-ENING AGENT IS GRATED ALMONDS, IN LIEU OF THE PINE NUTS MORE COMMONLY USED IN THE PESTO OF ITALY. USE FOR PASTA DISHES OF ALL KINDS, AND AS A SANDWICH SPREAD.

1 cup fresh basil leaves

¼ cup olive oil, or as needed

*3 tablespoons freshly grated Parmesan
   cheese*

*¼ cup coarsely chopped blanched
   almonds*

½ teaspoon salt

In a blender or in a food processor fitted with the metal blade, combine the basil leaves and ¼ cup olive oil. Purée until smooth. Add the cheese, almonds, and salt and process until all the ingredients are well blended into a sauce. If the sauce seems too thick, add a little more olive oil.

Use immediately or transfer to a bowl or jar with a tight-fitting lid and store in the refrigerator. It will keep for 3 to 4 days in the refrigerator.

SAUCE ROUGE

MAKES ABOUT ½ CUP

HERE IS AN AROMATIC SAUCE OF SUMMERTIME IN SOUTHERN FRANCE, REPLETE WITH THE TASTES OF SWEET RED PEPPERS, TOMATOES, AND GARLIC. IT IS USUALLY THICKENED WITH BREAD, BUT HERE I HAVE FOLLOWED A FRIEND'S VERSION, WHICH USES ALMONDS. I SERVE THIS SAUCE WITH SUMMER VEGETABLE DISHES OF ALL KINDS, AND WITH PASTA AND RICE.

Preheat a broiler, or prepare a fire in a charcoal or other grill.

Place the red pepper, tomatoes, and garlic cloves on a shallow pan and broil, turning once, until charred, 3 to 4 minutes on each side. Alternatively, place them on a grill rack (using a hinged basket for the garlic cloves) and grill, turning once until charred, 3 to 4 minutes on each side. Remove from the oven or grill rack and slip the pepper and the garlic into a plastic bag, seal it closed, and let stand for a few minutes to sweat and cool. Using your fingertips, peel away the skins from the pepper, then remove the stem, seeds, and ribs. Remove and discard the skins from the garlic. Peel off the skin and core the tomatoes.

In a blender or in a food processor fitted with the metal blade, combine the garlic cloves, almonds, and olive oil. Purée until smooth. Add the sweet pepper, tomatoes, salt, and black pepper and again purée until smooth.

Use immediately or transfer to a bowl or jar with a tight-fitting lid and store in the refrigerator. It will keep for 3 to 4 days.

1 large sweet red pepper

2 tomatoes

2 cloves garlic, unpeeled

2 teaspoons chopped blanched almonds

¼ cup olive oil

½ teaspoon salt

½ teaspoon freshly ground black pepper

TAPENADE

MAKES ABOUT 1 CUP

ALTHOUGH **TAPENADE** IS MORE OF A SPREAD THAN A SAUCE, IT IS SO USEFUL WITH VEGETABLES IT SEEMS A GOOD IDEA TO INCLUDE IT HERE. IT CAN BE MADE WITH GREEN OR BLACK OLIVES, SALTED OR BRINED, AND ALTHOUGH THE SPREAD TRADITIONALLY INCLUDES ANCHOVIES, IT IS QUITE SATISFYING WITHOUT THEM. IN MARKETS IN FRANCE, THERE ARE ALWAYS VENDORS SELLING TEN OR FIF-TEEN DIFFERENT KINDS OF OLIVES, SOME SPICED WITH GARLIC, OTHERS WITH FENNEL, LEMON, CHILIES, OR ONIONS. ANY OF THESE WOULD MAKE A GOOD **TAPENADE**. THE FINAL RESULT SHOULD BE BOTH SALTY AND TANGY, SO THE AMOUNT OF SALT YOU USE WILL DEPEND UPON THE TYPE OF OLIVES CHOSEN. THIS RECIPE WORKS ESPECIALLY WELL WITH MEDITERRANEAN-STYLE OLIVES. ◎ SPREAD **TAPENADE** ON TOASTS, USE IT TO TOP BITE-SIZED NEW POTATOES, COMBINE IT WITH SOFT CHEESE AS A FILLING FOR CRÊPES OR CANNELLONI, OR SERVE IT AS AN ACCOMPANIMENT TO RAW VEGETABLES OF ALL KINDS.

1 cup pitted green or black olives (about
   1 pound unpitted)

6 tablespoons olive oil

1 clove garlic

¼ cup drained capers

1 heaping tablespoon Dijon-style
   mustard

salt to taste

½ teaspoon fresh lemon juice (optional)

Traditionally, the olives and other ingredients are combined in a mortar and crushed, but a blender or a food processor fitted with the metal blade works well, too. Chop or crush the olives with 2 tablespoons of the olive oil and garlic. Add the capers and chop or crush again. Finally, add the mustard and the remaining 4 tablespoons olive oil and the optional lemon juice and mix to a paste. Taste and adjust for salt.

Use immediately or store in a tightly covered container in the refrigerator for up to 1 week.

HARISSA

MAKES ABOUT ½ CUP

MADE OF HOT PEPPERS, OLIVE OIL, SPICES, AND BROTH, **HARISSA** IS A STANDARD ACCOMPANI-
MENT TO COUSCOUS, A FAVORITE NORTH AFRICAN DISH ADOPTED BY THE FRENCH. STIRRED
IN AT THE LAST MINUTE, IT WILL ENLIVEN SOUPS OR STEWS AND MAKES A FINE SPREAD FOR GRILLED
OR BROILED VEGETABLES.

Remove and discard the stems and seeds from the dried chilies. Place the chilies
in a small grinder, such as a spice or coffee grinder, and grind until pulverized.
You should have a scant ¼ cup.

In a small bowl, using a fork, mash together the ground chili, garlic cloves,
cumin, turmeric, and salt to form a paste. Gradually stir in the olive oil until it is
incorporated. Then stir in the broth until it is fully combined.

Use immediately or store in a tightly covered container in the refrigerator for
up to 5 days.

*3 or 4 dried chili peppers, such
   as Anaheim*
8 cloves garlic
1 teaspoon ground cumin
1 teaspoon ground turmeric
½ teaspoon salt
4 tablespoons olive oil
*¼ cup Basic Vegetable Broth (page 22)
   or other vegetable broth*

TOMATO COULIS

MAKES ABOUT 3 CUPS

THIS **COULIS** IS ONE OF THE GREAT SUMMER SAUCES. KEEP IT ON HAND IN THE REFRIGERATOR TO USE ON PASTA, FOR POACHING, TO ADD TO SUMMER SOUPS OR STEWS, AND TO DRESS SUMMER VEGETABLES OF ALL KINDS, FROM STEAMED GREEN SNAP BEANS, ZUCCHINI, AND EGGPLANT TO CHOPPED WARM CHARD OR SPINACH. EXPERIMENT WITH USING MARVEL STRIPE, GREEN ZEBRA, GOLDEN JUBILEE, OR ANY OTHER SPECIALTY TOMATOES, AS LONG AS THEY ARE VERY RIPE. THE AMOUNT OF SUGAR NEEDED WILL DEPEND UPON WHETHER THE TOMATOES YOU USE ARE SWEET OR ACIDIC. ◉ TO MAKE OTHER TYPES OF **COULIS**, FINELY CHOP VEGETABLES—FENNEL, ONIONS, LEEKS, SWEET PEPPERS—AND THEN COOK THEM AS DESCRIBED HERE, BUT WITH THE ADDITION OF A LITTLE WATER OR BROTH. THE AMOUNT OF LIQUID AND THE LENGTH OF COOKING TIME NEEDED WILL VARY DEPENDING UPON THE VEGETABLE. A SWEET FRUIT **COULIS** CAN ALSO BE MADE. COOK DOWN SUCH FRUITS AS RASPBERRIES, KIWI FRUITS, AND PERSIMMONS WITH A LITTLE SUGAR, FRESH LEMON JUICE, AND WATER AND PERHAPS A SPRIG OF MINT, ROSEMARY, OR ANOTHER HERB, AND THEN PURÉE THE SAUCE.

5 pounds very ripe tomatoes (about 14 medium-sized)

2 tablespoons olive oil

1 clove garlic, crushed

½ teaspoon salt

½ teaspoon freshly ground black pepper

½ to 1 tablespoon sugar, if needed

1 tablespoon minced fresh thyme or basil

Peel the tomatoes by plunging them into boiling water for a second or two to loosen the skins, or by peeling them with a small knife, as you would a potato. Chop coarsely and set aside.

In a saucepan large enough to hold all the tomatoes at one time, warm the olive oil over medium heat. Add the garlic and sauté until softened, 2 or 3 minutes. Add the tomatoes and cook over low heat, stirring occasionally until thickened, about 45 minutes.

Taste the tomatoes and add the salt, pepper, and the sugar, if needed. Continue cooking until the sauce thickens, another 30 minutes to 1 hour. The timing will depend upon the meatiness of the tomatoes. Skim off any clear liquid that settles on top of the sauce and discard. Stir in the thyme or basil and simmer for another 10 minutes.

Use immediately, or let cool to room temperature. To store, transfer to a container with a tight-fitting lid and refrigerate for up to 5 days. Use at room temperature or reheated.

ONION CONFIT

MAKES ABOUT 4 CUPS

THIS IS A USEFUL PANTRY INGREDIENT TO USE NOT ONLY AS A SPREAD OR TOPPING FOR BREAD, BUT ALSO IN SOUPS, GRATINS, AND STEWS TO PROVIDE AN INTRIGUING UNDERLYING TASTE. COOKED SLOWLY IN BUTTER AND OLIVE OIL WITH BAY LEAVES, WINTER SAVORY, AND THYME, THE ONIONS CARAMELIZE, RELEASING THEIR NATURAL SUGARS AND BECOMING INFUSED WITH THE OTHER FLAVORS.

Preheat an oven to 300 degrees F.

Cut the butter into several chunks and put them on a large baking sheet. Place in the oven to melt, 4 or 5 minutes.

Remove the baking sheet from the oven and spread out the sliced onions on it. The layer of onions will be about 1 inch deep. Tuck the bay leaves amongst the onions, then sprinkle the onions with the thyme, savory, and pepper. Drizzle the olive oil evenly over the top.

Put the baking sheet back in the oven and cook the onions, turning them in the oil and butter every 10 or 15 minutes, until they have turned a light golden brown and have reduced in volume by nearly half, 1 to 1 ¼ hours.

Remove from the oven and let cool. Transfer to 1 or more clean, dry jars and cover tightly. Store in the refrigerator for up to 1 week.

4 tablespoons butter

4 pounds yellow or red onions, cut into slices ¼ to ⅜ inch thick (about 7 cups)

2 fresh or dried bay leaves

2 tablespoons fresh thyme leaves

1 tablespoon chopped fresh winter savory leaves

1 tablespoon freshly ground black pepper

¼ cup olive oil

INFUSED OILS AND VINEGARS

✳

THESE ARE OILS AND VINEGARS TO WHICH HERBS, FRUITS, OR SPICES HAVE BEEN ADDED AND THEN LEFT TO STAND LONG ENOUGH FOR THE LIQUID TO BECOME INFUSED WITH THEIR FLAVORS. THIS GENERALLY TAKES TEN TO FOURTEEN DAYS, BUT THE TIMING WILL DIFFER DEPENDING UPON THE INGREDIENTS. THE OILS ARE PARTICULARLY GOOD FOR MARINADES, VINAIGRETTES, AND ON THEIR OWN TO DRESS COOKED OR RAW VEGETABLES. THE VINEGARS ENHANCE VINAIGRETTES AND ARE A FRAGRANT MEDIUM FOR DEGLAZING PANS. INFUSED OILS AND VINEGARS SHOULD BE STORED IN A COOL, DARK PLACE — BETWEEN 34 AND 48 DEGREES F — OR IN THE REFRIGERATOR. IF THE OIL IS REFRIGERATED, BRING IT TO ROOM TEMPERATURE BEFORE USING.

ROSEMARY-INFUSED OLIVE OIL

MAKES ABOUT 2½ CUPS

PUNGENT AND RESINOUS, ROSEMARY READILY INFUSES OLIVE OIL TO PRODUCE AN EXCELLENT MARINADE AND BASTING SAUCE FOR GRILLED VEGETABLES, INCLUDING WINTER SQUASH, PARSNIPS, RADICCHIO, AND THE TRADITIONAL MEDITERRANEAN TRIO OF SUMMER SQUASH, EGGPLANT, AND SWEET PEPPERS. DRIZZLE IT OVER PIZZAS OR BREADS AND USE IT IN COOKING WHENEVER YOU WANT A SUBTLE ROSEMARY FLAVOR.

Crush the snipped rosemary slightly and put it in a clean, dry, wide-mouthed glass jar with a lid. Add the olive oil to cover the rosemary completely and then cover with the lid. Put the jar inside in a sunny window or outside in a sunny location. Let stand for about 10 days.

Taste the oil occasionally by pouring a little of it on a piece of bread. When the oil is sufficiently flavored—I sometimes leave mine for 3 weeks—remove the pieces of rosemary and discard them or use them for cooking. Strain the oil through a sieve lined with several layers of cheesecloth and decant it into a clean jar or bottle. Add a decorative sprig of fresh rosemary and seal with a cork or lid.

2 cups fresh rosemary sprigs, snipped
  into 1-inch lengths

2½ cups olive oil

1 fresh rosemary sprig, for the
  decanted oil

BLACK PEPPER–INFUSED OLIVE OIL

MAKES ABOUT 2½ CUPS

■ ■HIS OIL HAS A SMOOTH BITE OF PEPPER. I LIKE TO USE IT IN MARINADES OF ALL KINDS, FOR SAUTÉING VEGETABLES, AND IN VINAIGRETTES.

¼ *cup whole black peppercorns*
2 ½ *cups olive oil*

Crack the peppercorns and put them in a clean, dry glass jar with a lid. Pour in the olive oil. Steep and strain the oil as directed for Rosemary-Infused Olive Oil, preceding.

LEMON–INFUSED OLIVE OIL

MAKES ABOUT 2½ CUPS

A LIGHT, FRUITY TASTE OF CITRUS MAKES THIS OIL A GOOD PARTNER FOR BOTH SPRING AND WINTER VEGETABLES, SUCH AS ASPARAGUS, ARTICHOKES, CELERY ROOT, TURNIPS, AND RADICCHIO. USE IT AS A MARINADE, IN A VINAIGRETTE WITH LEMON JUICE, OR TO DRESS SALADS ON ITS OWN.

1 ½ *pounds lemons*
3 *fresh or dried bay leaves*
2 ½ *cups olive oil*

Cut the lemons into quarters and put them and the bay leaves in a clean, dry wide-mouthed glass jar with a lid, large enough to hold the olive oil eventually. Cover the jar, put it in a cool place, and let stand for 24 hours. The next day, pour the olive oil over the lemons, cover the jar, and let stand for 3 or 4 days.

Taste the oil. If it tastes sufficiently lemony, remove and discard the lemons and bay leaves. If not, let it stand for another 3 or 4 days, and then discard the lemons and bay leaves. When the oil is ready, strain it through a sieve lined with several layers of cheesecloth. Decant the oil into a clean jar or bottle and seal with a cork or lid.

TARRAGON VINEGAR

MAKES 4 CUPS

USE THIS CLASSIC VINEGAR WITH CITRUS FRUITS AND SPICY INGREDIENTS SUCH AS WATER-CRESS, AND TO DEGLAZE PAN JUICES IN PLACE OF WHITE WINE.

Crush the snipped tarragon slightly and put it into a clean, dry wide-mouthed glass jar with a lid. Pour in the vinegar and cover with the lid. Place the jar inside in a sunny window or outside in a sunny location. Let stand for 10 to 14 days.

When the vinegar has become infused with the flavor of the herbs to your satisfaction, remove and discard the tarragon sprigs. Strain the vinegar through a sieve lined with several layers of cheesecloth. Decant it into clean, dry bottles. If you wish, add a sprig or two of fresh tarragon, although after a few weeks they may begin to deteriorate and should be removed. Store in a cool, dark place. The vinegar will keep for up to 1 year.

1 cup fresh tarragon sprigs, snipped into 1-inch lengths

4 cups distilled white wine vinegar

1 or 2 fresh tarragon sprigs, for the decanted vinegar

WILD BERRY VINEGAR

MAKES 3 CUPS

BLACKBERRIES, BLACK CURRANTS, RED CURRANTS, RASPBERRIES, OR ANY MIXTURE OF SUMMER SOFT FRUITS WILL RESULT IN A TART-SWEET VINEGAR THAT IS PARTICULARLY WONDERFUL WITH FRUIT SALADS OR TO HEIGHTEN THE TASTE OF SUMMER FRUIT DESSERTS. IT IS A GOOD CHOICE, TOO, FOR DEGLAZING PAN JUICES FROM SWEET VEGETABLES, SUCH AS PARSNIPS, LEEKS, ONIONS, AND SHALLOTS.

1 cup very ripe wild or cultivated berries
3 cups red wine vinegar

Put the berries in a clean, dry wide-mouthed glass jar with a lid. Pour in the vinegar, cover with the lid, and proceed as directed for Tarragon Vinegar, preceding.

BASIL VINEGAR

MAKES 3 1/2 CUPS

PURPLE OR GREEN BASIL MAY BE USED FOR MAKING THIS VINEGAR. THE PURPLE VARIETY IMPARTS NOT ONLY ITS FLAVOR BUT ALSO ITS COLOR TO THE VINEGAR, RESULTING IN A SOFT BURGUNDY SHADE, WHILE THE GREEN BASIL LEAVES ONLY THE SLIGHTEST HINT OF YELLOW-GREEN. USE THE BASIL VINEGAR ON TOMATOES, ON SALADS MADE WITH RICE OR PASTA, OR IN COMBINATION WITH SUMMER VEGETABLES.

1 cup loosely packed green or purple basil
    leaves
3 ½ cups distilled white wine vinegar

Crush the basil slightly between your fingertips just enough to begin releasing the volatile oils, and put it in a clean, dry wide-mouthed glass jar with a lid. Pour in the vinegar, cover with the lid, and proceed as directed for Tarragon Vinegar, preceding.

NASTURTIUM BLOSSOM VINEGAR

MAKES 3½ CUPS

PEPPERY NASTURTIUM BLOSSOMS ARE USED TO MAKE THIS VINEGAR, WHICH ENHANCES SPICY GREENS. I LIKE IT FOR SALAD OF WILD GREENS (PAGE 56) AND TO POUR OVER LITTLE POTATOES THAT I SERVE AS PART OF A **CRUDITÉ** PLATE.

Put the nasturtiums in a clean, dry wide-mouthed glass jar with a lid. Pour in the vinegar, cover with the lid, and proceed as directed for Tarragon Vinegar, preceding.

1 cup loosely packed, pesticide-free nasturtium blossoms

3 ½ cups distilled white wine vinegar

CHAPTER TWO

APPETIZERS
& SMALL
DISHES

APPETIZERS & SMALL DISHES

❋

IN FRANCE, EVEN THOUGH LIFESTYLES AND TRADITIONS HAVE CHANGED DRAMATICALLY OVER THE LAST TWENTY YEARS, IT IS STILL COMMON IN MOST FAMILIES AND RESTAURANTS TO HAVE AT LEAST A THREE-COURSE MEAL. The *entrée*, or appetizer course, may be as plain as a plate of *crudités*, a collection of raw vegetables and vegetable salads that might include grated carrots, pickled beets, and sliced cucumbers, or a slice of winter keeper melon. It can be the star course, showcasing a seasonal specialty such as the first young, tender artichokes or a summer soup of ripe tomatoes. It might be as substantial as braised brussels sprouts, or meant for lingering over, such as a whole roasted garlic head served with fresh cheese and lots of bread.

The appetizer sets the tone for the meal that follows, and its taste should entice and beckon one on to the main course, even if the *entrée* is as unassuming as warm leeks in vinaigrette. Well-chosen fresh ingredients, treated simply, will rarely disappoint.

SHREDDED CARROT AND ONION SALAD

SERVES 3 OR 4

IAM A BIG FAN OF THE OLD-FASHIONED **CRUDITÉ** STILL SERVED IN MODEST, WORKING CLASS RESTAU-RANTS THROUGHOUT FRANCE. I WILL PASS OVER FINE-SOUNDING FIRST COURSES OF COMPOSED DISHES, OPTING INSTEAD FOR A SIMPLE PLATTER CONSISTING OF **CARROTTE RAPÉ, CELERI RAVE REMOULADE, SALADE DE POMMES DE TERRE,** A FEW PIECES OF QUARTERED HARD-BOILED EGG AND A SCATTERING OF OLIVES. THE ACTUAL MAKE-UP OF THE PLATTER VARIES AND MAY INCLUDE **PÂTE,** FENNEL, MUSHROOMS, OR OTHER TASTES, BUT IT IS THE BASIC LITTLE INDIVIDUALLY DRESSED SALADS THAT DELIGHT ME.

Grate the carrots and the onion into a shallow serving dish. Drizzle with the vinaigrette and toss to coat evenly. Garnish with the olives, if using, and serve.

4 large carrots, peeled

¼ yellow, white, or red onion

¼ to ⅓ cup Classic Vinaigrette (page 24) or other vinaigrette

6 salt-cured black or green olives (optional)

CREAMY CELERY ROOT AND BARLEY SOUP

SERVES 4 OR 5

THIS IS A RICHLY FLAVORED COUNTRY SOUP THAT WARMS YOU FROM THE TOES UP WITH EACH SPOONFUL. BARLEY IS TRADITIONALLY CULTIVATED IN NORTHERN FRANCE, WHERE IT WILL MATURE IN THE RELATIVELY SHORT GROWING SEASON; CELERY ROOT IS A FAIRLY COLD-HARDY VEGETABLE THAT ALSO STORES WELL. THUS, WE FIND THE MARRIAGE OF THE **TERROIR** HERE.

¼ cup pearl barley

4 cups water

½ teaspoon salt

2 tablespoons butter

1 leek, including the tender portion of the green tops, minced

¾ to 1 large celery root, peeled and cut into 1-inch dice (about 3 cups)

3 cups Leek and Mushroom Broth (page 20) or other vegetable broth

½ cup half-and-half

½ cup milk

In a saucepan, combine the barley with 3 cups of the water and the salt. Bring to a boil, cover, reduce the heat to low, and simmer until tender, 1 to 1 ½ hours. Drain the barley and set aside.

In a heavy-bottomed saucepan over medium heat, melt the butter. When it begins to foam, add the leek and celery root and sauté until the color changes slightly, 3 to 4 minutes. Add the broth and the remaining 1 cup water. Bring to a boil, reduce the heat to low, and simmer, uncovered, until the celery root is tender, 15 to 20 minutes. Remove from the heat.

Transfer half of the soup to a blender or to a food processor fitted with the metal blade and roughly purée it. Return the purée to the saucepan and place over medium heat. Add the cooked barley, the half-and-half, and milk, stir well, and heat to serving temperature. Do not allow the soup to boil.

Ladle into warmed bowls and serve piping hot.

CELERY ROOT AND POTATO PURÉE

SERVES 4

THE DISTINCTIVE, SHARP FLAVOR OF CELERY ROOT BLENDED WITH THE EARTHY TASTE OF POTA-
TOES AND THE RICHNESS OF MILK AND BUTTER IS AS COMFORTING A DISH AS ONE COULD WANT. I
HAVE OFTEN COME IN AFTER A LONG DAY OF WORK, AND STAYED ON MY FEET JUST A LITTLE BIT
LONGER TO PREPARE THIS PURÉE. IT MAKES A FINE FIRST COURSE, BUT IT CAN ALSO BE SERVED AS AN
ACCOMPANIMENT TO OTHER DISHES, SUCH AS DEEP-DISH **CASSOULET** OF FLAGEOLET BEANS (PAGE 124),
RAGOUT OF WILD MUSHROOMS (PAGE 110), OR VEGETABLE **POT AU FEU** (PAGE 125), OR USED TO TOP
OTHER DISHES, SUCH AS GLACÉ CARROTS, SHALLOTS, AND FENNEL (PAGE 89).

Peel the potatoes (or leave unpeeled, if you prefer) and cut them into 1-inch cubes.

Place the potatoes in a large saucepan with water to cover and 1 teaspoon of the salt. Bring to a boil over high heat and boil, uncovered, for 10 minutes. Add the celery root and boil for another 10 minutes.

Drain the potatoes and celery root and return to the hot saucepan. Add ¼ cup of the milk and, using a hand masher or electric beater, purée the vegetables, adding more milk if necessary to achieve the proper consistency.

Season with the remaining ½ teaspoon salt and the pepper and stir in the butter. Serve at once.

6 medium-sized baking or boiling
  potatoes
1 ½ teaspoons salt
1 large celery root, peeled and cut into
  1-inch cubes
¼ to ½ cup milk
½ teaspoon freshly ground black pepper
2 tablespoons butter

GARDEN POTAGE

SERVES 4

AT THE RESTAURANTS OF SMALL COUNTRY HOTELS WHERE **DEMI-PENSION** OR **PENSION** (HALF OR FULL BOARD) IS AVAILABLE WITH THE ROOM, ONE STILL FINDS SOME VERSION OF GARDEN POTAGE SERVED AS THE FIRST COURSE. IN THE PAST, THE VEGETABLES CAME DIRECTLY FROM THE HOTEL'S VEGETABLE GARDEN. THE SOUP IS NO MORE THAN THE SIMPLE SIMMERING OF SEASONAL VEGETABLES IN WATER OR BROTH, WHICH IS THEN PURÉED. THIS VERSION INCORPORATES SPRING VEGETABLES, BUT A SUMMER SOUP MIGHT COMBINE ZUCCHINI AND GREEN SNAP BEANS INSTEAD OF RADISHES AND CARROTS. LEEKS OR ONIONS ARE ALMOST ALWAYS INCLUDED FOR FLAVOR, ESPECIALLY IF WATER INSTEAD OF BROTH IS USED, AND POTATOES ARE GENERALLY ADDED TO THICKEN THE SOUP, ALTHOUGH RICE, PASTA, OR EVEN BREAD WOULD ALSO WORK WELL.

½ head butter lettuce

2 carrots, peeled

5 radishes with leaves intact

4 or 5 new potatoes (about ¾ pound), unpeeled

4 or 5 green onions, including the tender portion of the green tops

1 tablespoon butter

2 cups water, Basic Vegetable Broth (page 22), or other vegetable broth

¼ cup chopped fresh parsley

½ to 1 teaspoon salt, or to taste

½ cup cooked white rice or small pasta (optional)

Coarsely chop the lettuce, carrots, radishes and their leaves, potatoes, and green onions. In a heavy-bottomed saucepan with a tight-fitting lid, melt the butter over medium heat. When it begins to foam, add all the chopped vegetables and stir well. Cover and cook for 2 to 3 minutes, then reduce the heat to low and continue to cook covered until the vegetables have softened and the leaves wilted, another 4 to 5 minutes.

Uncover, add the water or broth, parsley, and, if using water, the salt. Cover and continue to cook over low heat for 15 minutes, stirring occasionally.

Using a hand beater, a food mill, or a food processor fitted with the metal blade, purée the soup. Taste and adjust the seasoning. Return the puréed soup to the saucepan (if a hand beater has not been used) and add the rice or pasta, if using. Heat to serving temperature.

Ladle into warmed bowls and serve hot.

FRESH PEA SOUP WITH CRÈME FRAÎCHE AND CHIVE BLOSSOMS

ONE OF THE FIRST CROPS I GREW WHEN I LIVED IN FRANCE WAS PEAS. I PLANTED ABOUT HALF AN ACRE OF THEM AND I AM NOT REALLY SURE WHY. IT MIGHT BE BECAUSE THE SEEDS WERE AVAILABLE IN HUGE BAGS AT THE LITTLE GRAIN-AND-FEED STORE AND THEY WERE CHEAP. THE PLANTS WERE BEAUTIFUL AND MET ALL MY EXPECTATIONS OF HAVING AN ENTIRE FIELD OF SOMETHING. STARTING WITH THE FIRST PODS BARELY PLUMPED WITH TINY PEAS, I PICKED KILOS AND KILOS OF THEM, FINISHING WITH THE LARGE PODS FULLY ROUNDED WITH BIG, STARCHY SPECIMENS. MY NEIGHBOR TOLD ME THAT THE MATURE PEAS ARE BEST FOR SOUP, BEING TOO BIG AND TOUGH TO STEAM AND BUTTER SIMPLY, AS I HAD PREPARED THE SMALL, YOUNG PEAS.

Shell the peas and set aside, reserving the pods. In a saucepan, bring the vegetable broth to a boil. Add the pods and the water, cover, and reduce the heat to medium-low. Simmer until the flavor has been extracted from the pods, 15 to 20 minutes. Strain, discarding the pods.

Return the broth to the saucepan and add the shelled peas. Bring to a boil, cover, reduce the heat to medium-low, and cook the peas until they are tender. This will take anywhere from 15 to 40 minutes, depending upon the size and maturity of the peas.

When the peas are ready, transfer the soup to a blender or to a food processor fitted with a metal blade and, working in batches if necessary, purée until smooth. Return the purée to the saucepan, add the salt and pepper, and heat to serving temperature but do not boil.

Ladle the soup into warmed bowls and garnish each serving with a little *crème fraîche* and a sprinkling of chive blossoms or chives. Serve immediately.

2 pounds English peas in their pods

3 cups Leek and Mushroom Broth (page 20) or other vegetable broth

½ cup water

½ teaspoon salt

½ teaspoon freshly ground black pepper

2 tablespoons crème fraîche

2 tablespoons minced fresh chive blossoms or chives

TOMATO–TARRAGON SOUP WITH FENNEL CROUTONS

SERVES 4

TARRAGON SUBTLY FLAVORS THIS GARDEN-FRESH SUMMERTIME TOMATO SOUP, GIVING IT A SURPRISE FINISH THAT IS HEIGHTENED BY THE CRUNCH OF TOASTED FENNEL SEEDS. TARRAGON IS EASY TO GROW EVEN IN A SMALL WINDOWSILL GARDEN. IT IS A CLASSIC INGREDIENT IN FRENCH COOKING AND JUST A FEW SNIPPETS CAN ADD FLAVOR TO EGG, CHEESE, AND VEGETABLE DISHES.

For the soup:

4 to 5 pounds very ripe tomatoes
  (13 or 14 medium-sized)
1 tablespoon butter
2 shallots, thinly sliced
4 tablespoons minced fresh tarragon
½ cup dry white wine
4 cups water
½ teaspoon salt

For the croutons:

½ loaf day-old baguette or similar
  bread
3 tablespoons olive oil
1 tablespoon fennel seeds
5 whole black peppercorns
¼ teaspoon salt

To make the soup, first peel the tomatoes by plunging them into boiling water for a second or two to loosen the skins, or by peeling them with a small knife as you would a potato. Halve the tomatoes and remove the seeds, then chop the tomatoes coarsely, capturing their juices.

In a large heavy-bottomed saucepan over medium heat, melt the butter. When it begins to foam, add the shallots and sauté until translucent, 3 or 4 minutes. Add ¾ cup of the chopped tomatoes and their juices and 2 tablespoons of the tarragon. Cook over medium heat, stirring occasionally, until the color of the tomatoes changes and they have softened somewhat, about 10 minutes. Add the wine and bring the mixture to a boil. Reduce the heat to low and simmer, uncovered, until reduced to about ½ cup. This should take about 20 minutes.

Add the remaining tomatoes and their juices, the water, and salt. Increase the heat to medium-low and cook until the soup has reduced to about 6 cups, 20 to 30 minutes. While soup simmers make the croutons. Preheat oven to 350 degrees F.

Cut the bread into 1-inch-thick slices, then cut each slice in half. Place the slices on a baking sheet and brush the tops with the olive oil. Place the fennel seeds in a bowl and bruise them with the back of a wooden spoon. Grind or crush the peppercorns and add them and the salt to the fennel. Gently press this mixture into the bread with the back of a wooden spoon or your fingertips.

Bake the bread slices until they are slightly golden, about 15 minutes. Remove and set aside until the soup is ready.

Just before serving, stir the remaining 2 tablespoons tarragon into the soup and simmer for 2 to 3 minutes. Ladle the soup into a warmed terrine or individual bowls and float the croutons on top. Serve at once.

YELLOW TOMATO–GINGER SOUP

SERVES 4

GINGER AND TURMERIC PROVIDE A SHARP, CLEAN TASTE THAT COMPLEMENTS THE SWEETNESS OF SIMMERED LATE-SEASON TOMATOES AND ADDS AN EXOTIC ACCENT. CILANTRO AND FRESH TARRAGON STIRRED IN AT THE END OF THE COOKING HEIGHTEN THE FLAVOR COMBINATIONS. A GRILLED BREAD ROUND, RESTING IN THE BOTTOM OF EACH BOWL, SOAKS UP THE GOLDEN SOUP AND GIVES SUBSTANCE TO EVERY RICH MOUTHFUL. THIS SOUP WOULD BE GOOD FOLLOWED BY FLUFFY BREAD AND YELLOW ZUCCHINI **TIAN** (PAGE 112) OR CHARD AND POTATO TERRINE (PAGE 118).

2 ½ pounds yellow tomatoes
    (about 5 large)

1 tablespoon butter

2 cloves garlic

2 tablespoons minced fresh ginger

½ yellow onion, very thinly sliced

½ teaspoon salt

½ teaspoon ground cumin

¼ teaspoon ground turmeric

⅛ teaspoon cayenne pepper

⅛ teaspoon freshly ground black pepper

1 ⅔ cups Leek and Mushroom Broth
    (see page 20) or other vegetable broth

8 large slices country-style bread

¼ cup chopped fresh cilantro

¼ cup chopped fresh tarragon

Peel the tomatoes by plunging them into boiling water for a second or two to loosen the skins, or by peeling them with a small knife, as you would a potato. Halve the tomatoes and remove the seeds, then chop the tomatoes. Set aside.

In a heavy-bottomed saucepan over medium-low heat, melt the butter. Mince 1 of the garlic cloves and add to the pan, along with the ginger. Sauté for 2 to 3 minutes until softened. Add the onion, increase the heat to medium, and sauté until the onion is translucent, another 2 to 3 minutes. Add the tomatoes and cook, stirring, for 4 or 5 minutes. Stir in the salt, cumin, turmeric, cayenne pepper, and black pepper, and then pour in the broth. Reduce the heat to low and simmer, uncovered, for 10 to 15 minutes to blend the flavors.

While the soup is simmering, preheat a broiler. Place the bread slices on a broiler pan and slip under the broiler until lightly browned, 3 to 4 minutes. Turn and broil until browned on the second side, 3 to 4 minutes longer. (Alternatively, grill over a charcoal fire for about the same amount of time.) Remove from the broiler and rub 1 side of each grilled bread slice with the remaining garlic clove.

To serve, put a piece of the bread in the bottom of each warmed individual bowl and ladle the soup over it. Top each serving with a sprinkling of cilantro and tarragon and pass the remaining bread.

CRISPY TWICE-COOKED NEW POTATOES WITH MIXED SAUTÉED GREENS

SERVES 4

THE SECOND COOKING SEALS THE POTATOES AND FORMS A CRUNCHY OUTER CRUST, LEAVING THE INSIDE MOIST AND SUCCULENT. WHEN COMBINED WITH THE LIVELY FLAVORS OF MIXED SAUTÉED GREENS, THE POTATOES BECOME A VERY SATISFYING DISH.

5 or 6 medium-sized fine-fleshed boiling potatoes, such as Yukon Gold, Yellow Finn, or White Rose

Salt to taste, plus ¾ teaspoon salt

4 tablespoons olive oil or Rosemary-Infused Olive Oil (page 37)

4 tablespoons butter

½ yellow onion, chopped

1 clove garlic, chopped

2 tablespoons minced fresh chives

2 tablespoons minced fresh parsley

4 cups assorted sturdy, young greens, such as kale, red and green chard, beet tops, escarole, and spinach, in any combination, coarsely chopped

1 teaspoon freshly ground black pepper

Peel the potatoes (or leave unpeeled, if you prefer) and cut them into 1-inch cubes. Place the potatoes in a saucepan with water to cover and add salt to taste. Bring to a boil and cook, uncovered, until tender and easily pierced with the tip of a knife, about 20 minutes. Drain and set aside. (This step can be done well in advance of the second cooking.)

For the second cooking, combine 3 tablespoons of the oil and 3 tablespoons of the butter in a large skillet and place over medium heat. When they begin to foam, add the onion and garlic and sauté until translucent, 3 or 4 minutes. Add the potatoes and sprinkle them with ½ teaspoon of the salt. Cook until they are crisp and golden on one side, 7 or 8 minutes.

Turn the potatoes with a spatula and fry until golden, 6 or 7 minutes longer. Sprinkle them with the chives and parsley.

To sauté the greens, put the remaining 1 tablespoon each butter and olive oil in a large skillet over low heat. When the butter and oil begin to foam, add the greens, cover, and cook for 1 to 2 minutes. Uncover and stir the greens. They should be wilted but still retain their bright color. Sprinkle with the remaining ¼ teaspoon salt and the pepper.

Spoon the potatoes onto a warmed serving plate and arrange the greens alongside. Serve at once.

SALAD OF WILD GREENS

SERVES 4 OR 5

COME SPRING IN FRANCE, ALL SORTS OF WILD GREENS ARE GATHERED AND USED FOR MAKING SALADS. SOME OF THE GREENS, LIKE YOUNG DANDELION AND THE CHICORIES, ARE BITTER, WHILE OTHERS, SUCH AS PURSLANE AND LAMB'S LETTUCE, ARE QUITE MILD. THESE SALADS ARE CONSIDERED A TRUE SPECIALTY OF THE SEASON, AND IT IS NOT UNUSUAL FOR GUESTS TO COME EARLY TO SUNDAY LUNCH IN THE COUNTRY TO HAVE THE PLEASURE OF HELPING TO GATHER THE SALAD GREENS. ❀ IF YOU ARE NOT FAMILIAR WITH THE EDIBLE WILD GREENS IN YOUR AREA, TRY PURCHASING YOUNG CULTIVATED GREENS AT A LOCAL FARMER'S MARKET. TALK WITH THE FARMERS ABOUT WILD GREENS, TOO, AS THEY ARE OFTEN QUITE KNOWLEDGEABLE.

4 cups assorted edible wild greens, or a mixture of specialty salad greens that includes arugula, radicchio, young lettuces, and frisée

½ to ¾ cup Garlic Vinaigrette (page 24) or other vinaigrette

2 hard-cooked eggs, chopped (optional)

Wash and clean the greens carefully, discarding any old, dead, or bruised leaves. If using dandelion greens, trim and chop the root and use it as well. Dry the greens thoroughly in a salad spinner or with a towel.

Put ½ cup of the vinaigrette in a large salad bowl. Add the greens and turn them with your hands or a large spoon until they are well coated. Garnish with the chopped eggs, if desired, and serve at once.

GRILLED GOAT FETA IN GRAPE LEAVES WITH TOMATO BITS

SERVES 4

EACH BITEFUL OF THESE PACKETS BRIMS WITH THE CHARACTER OF THE **TERROIR** OF PROVENCE'S DRY UPPER REACHES, WHERE THE GOATS FEED ON JUNIPER, WILD THYME, AND WINTER SAVORY AND THE GRAPEVINES GROW IN GRAVELLY RED SOIL. ON THE GRILL, ALL OF THE FRAGRANT FLAVORS MERGE.

Prepare a fire in a charcoal or other grill.

Remove the stems and any large veins from the fresh or jarred grape leaves. Cut the cheese into 1-inch squares about ½ inch thick. Place 1 leaf shiny side down on a work surface. Put a tomato half, cut side up, on the leaf. Top with a square of cheese and then with another tomato half, cut side down. Fold the leaf around the cheese and tomato, bringing the bottom edge up first, then a side, followed by the top edge, and finally the remaining side. Secure with a toothpick. Set aside, folded side down. Repeat with the remaining leaves, cheese, and tomatoes.

Place the leaf packets folded side down on the grill rack. Cook for 45 seconds to 1 minute. Turn over the packets and cook just long enough for the leaves to change from bright green to olive and for the cheese inside to warm and begin to melt, about 45 seconds longer.

Arrange on a platter or individual plates and serve hot or warm.

12 young, tender, fresh or jarred grape leaves, each about the size of a hand

½ pound goat's milk feta or other dry goat's milk cheese

12 cherry tomatoes, halved

PROVENÇAL TOMATOES

SERVES 6 TO 8

SWEET, SUN-RIPENED TOMATOES TOPPED WITH SPRINKLINGS OF GARLIC, OLIVE OIL, BREAD CRUMBS, AND **HERBES DE PROVENCE** AND THEN WARMED TO BUBBLING BENEATH THE BROILER ARE SERVED BY THE PLATTERFUL DURING SUMMERS IN PROVENCE. OFFER THEM AS A FIRST COURSE PRECEDING, FOR EXAMPLE, VEGETABLE SOUP WITH **PISTOU** (PAGE 91) OR CANNELLONI FILLED WITH DANDELION GREENS AND MUSHROOMS (PAGE 99), OR AS AN ACCOMPANIMENT TO A MAIN DISH, PERHAPS **GNOCCHI** WITH GORGONZOLA AND WINTER SAVORY (PAGE 268) OR CHARD AND PARSLEY QUICHE WITH TWO CHEESES (PAGE 121).

8 medium-sized tomatoes,
    halved crosswise

3 cloves garlic, minced

¼ cup fine dried bread crumbs

2 teaspoons salt

¼ cup herbes de Provence

¼ cup olive oil

Preheat a broiler.

Place the tomatoes cut side up on a baking sheet. Sprinkle the garlic, bread crumbs, salt, and *herbes de Provence* evenly over the tomatoes. Then drizzle a little of the olive oil over the top of each. Place the baking sheet under the broiler and broil until the tomatoes have softened and the topping has browned slightly, 4 or 5 minutes.

Serve hot or at room temperature.

YOUNG SQUASH & THEIR BLOSSOMS WITH GREEN RICE FILLING

SERVES 3 OR 4

FRENCH MARKET VEGETABLE VENDORS SELL STEMS OF BRIGHT GOLD MALE SQUASH BLOSSOMS AND SOMETIMES VERY YOUNG SQUASH WITH **LES FLEURS** STILL ATTACHED IN THE SUMMERTIME. THE BLOSSOMS ARE TUCKED FULL WITH A STUFFING, THEN BRIEFLY BAKED OR SAUTÉED. BECAUSE THE SQUASH AND THEIR FLOWERS ARE SO FRESH AND TENDER, THE DISH REQUIRES VERY LITTLE COOKING, YET IT IS INTENSELY FLAVORFUL. AND WHEN THE BLOSSOMS COME DIRECTLY FROM YOUR GARDEN TO THE KITCHEN, CUT ONLY MOMENTS FROM THE VINE, THIS SIMPLE COUNTRY DISH BECOMES STELLAR.

In a saucepan over medium heat, melt the butter with the olive oil. When they begin to foam, add the onion and sauté until translucent, 2 to 3 minutes. Add the rice and sauté until the rice glistens and begins to become slightly opaque, another 2 to 3 minutes. Add the water, salt, parsley, and half of the basil and bring to a boil. Cover, reduce the heat to low, and simmer until the rice is tender and all of the water is absorbed, about 20 minutes. Remove from the heat and, using a fork, stir in the remaining basil. Set aside, covered.

To fill the blossoms, with or without the squash attached, open each flower gently and spoon in about 1 ½ tablespoons of the rice mixture. It should reach to the point on the blossom where the petals begin to separate into points. Fold the points, overlapping them, over the filling. Gently secure the fold with a tooth-pick. Place the stuffed blossoms upright, folded side down, on a flat plate. Continue in this manner until all the blossoms are filled. Reserve any leftover rice for another use.

In a large skillet, warm the *Coulis* over medium heat. When it is hot, add the blossoms with or without the squash attached and cover the skillet. Cook over medium heat for 3 to 4 minutes. Reduce the heat to low and cook for 2 to 3 minutes longer if you are using only the blossoms, and 4 to 5 minutes longer if the squash are attached. The squash should be just barely tender when pierced with a knife. Do not overcook.

Place on individual plates and serve hot or at room temperature with the sauce spooned over the top.

1 tablespoon butter

1 tablespoon olive oil

2 tablespoons minced yellow onion or shallot

⅔ cup long-grain white rice

1 ⅓ cups water

½ teaspoon salt

¼ cup minced fresh parsley

¼ cup minced fresh basil

12 small zucchini or other summer squash, with blossoms attached, or male blossoms

1 cup Tomato Coulis (page 34)

GRILLED RADICCHIO WITH BALSAMIC VINAIGRETTE

SERVES 4 OR 5

RADICCHIO AT THE MARKET LOOKS LIKE A SMALL HEAD OF BRIGHT MAGENTA CABBAGE WITH WHITE RIBS. WHEN GROWN IN THE GARDEN OR FIELD, HOWEVER, THE HEADS ARE USUALLY SUR-ROUNDED BY HUGE, DARK GREEN, RED-RIBBED OUTER LEAVES THAT PROTECT THEM FROM THE DAMAG-ING COLD AND FREEZES THAT ALSO TENDERIZE AND SWEETEN THEM. FARMERS IN FRANCE AND ITALY HAVE PROUDLY SHOWED ME FIELDS FULL OF BLACK LUMPS. EACH LUMP WAS COVERED WITH LAYERS OF WITHERED, FROST-KILLED LEAVES THAT, WHEN PEELED BACK, REVEALED GLOWING JEWELLIKE HEADS OF RADICCHIO. ❀ WHEN GRILLED OR OTHERWISE COOKED, RADICCHIO LOSES ITS GLORIOUS HUE AND TURNS BROWN, BUT IT TASTES SO GOOD NO ONE MISSES THE COLOR. THE SWEETNESS OF THE BALSAMIC VINEGAR INCREASES THE BITTERSWEET FLAVOR OF RADICCHIO, AS DOES THE SMOKY TASTE FROM THE GRILL. SERVE WITH FRESH GOAT CHEESE AND COUNTRY BREAD AS A FIRST COURSE, OR OMIT THE CHEESE AND SERVE AS AN ACCOMPANIMENT TO A MAIN COURSE SUCH AS **TIAN** OF CELERY ROOT, TURNIP, FEN-NEL, AND RUTABAGA (PAGE 90) OR **GNOCCHI** WITH GORGONZOLA AND WINTER SAVORY (PAGE 268).

2 firm heads radicchio
   (about ¾ pound each)
¼ cup olive oil
1 tablespoon fresh thyme leaves
¼ teaspoon salt
½ teaspoon freshly ground black pepper
½ cup Balsamic Vinaigrette (page 26)

Cut each radicchio head from the top through the stem into 3 or 4 slices each about ½ inch thick. Try to ensure that each slice has a bit of the stem end, as this helps to hold the slices together on the grill. In a small bowl, whisk together the olive oil, thyme, salt, and pepper. Arrange half of the radicchio slices in a single layer in a shallow baking dish and pour half of the olive oil mixture evenly over them. Top with the remaining radicchio slices and pour the remaining olive oil mixture evenly over them. Let the radicchio marinate for at least 1 hour or as long as 4 hours at room temperature.

Prepare a fire in a charcoal or other grill. When the fire is medium-hot, place the radicchio slices on the grill rack and cook until they are browned but not charred on the first side, 2 to 3 minutes. Turn them over and grill on the second side until browned, 2 to 3 minutes.

Remove to a platter or individual serving plates. Drizzle with the Balsamic Vinaigrette and serve warm.

ARTICHOKES STUFFED WITH FENNEL DUXELLES

COME SPRING AND EARLY SUMMER, THE MARKETS OF PROVENCE AND NORMANDY ARE FULL OF SMALL, YOUNG ARTICHOKES. THE ARTICHOKES ARE GATHERED, STILL ON THEIR STEMS, INTO **BOTTES** OF FOUR OR FIVE AND SOLD BY THE BUNDLE AS A SEASONAL SPECIALTY. THESE ARE SO YOUNG, THE FURRY THISTLED HEART HAS NOT YET DEVELOPED, AND EXCEPT FOR A FEW OUTER LEAVES AND THORNY TIPS, THE ENTIRE ARTICHOKE MAY BE EATEN. FILLED WITH A FINE **DUXELLES** AND FINISHED BY A SHORT BAKING IN A LEMONY OLIVE OIL, THE TINY ARTICHOKES MAKE PERFECT BITE-SIZED HORS D'OEUVRES. IF YOU ARE FORTUNATE ENOUGH TO HAVE ARTICHOKES GROWING IN YOUR GARDEN, HARVEST SOME OF THEM VERY YOUNG AND TREAT THEM AS A DELICACY.

To prepare the artichokes, pour the water into a large bowl and add the vinegar. Working with one artichoke at a time, trim off the upper third of the small ones and up to one-half of the larger, more mature ones. Cut off each stem even with the base. Peel or cut away the outer leaves until you reach the inner, tender leaves, which are yellowish green. Gently pull apart the leaves to reveal the center and, using a small, pointed spoon, scoop out the center to make room for the stuffing. The more mature artichokes will have a partially developed thistle, which you must take care to remove entirely. As each artichoke is trimmed, slip it into the bowl of acidulated water to prevent discoloring.

When all of the artichokes have been trimmed, drain them and place on a steamer over boiling water. Cover and steam until they are tender when pierced with the tip of a sharp knife. The length of time required will depend upon the size and maturity of the artichokes; the small artichokes will take about 15 to 20 minutes, while the larger ones will take about 45 minutes.

Meanwhile, preheat an oven to 350 degrees F.

Mince as many shallots as needed to measure about ¼ cup. Trim the fennel bulb, discarding any tough or discolored outer leaves and cutting away any stalks and feathery tops. Mince enough of the bulb to measure about ½ cup (reserve any remaining fennel for another use). Mince the mushrooms, including the stems.

In a small skillet or saucepan over medium heat, melt the butter. When it begins to foam, add the shallots and sauté until translucent, 2 to 3 minutes. Then

4 cups water

¼ cup distilled white or other vinegar

12 small, 6 medium-sized, or 4 large
    artichokes

3 or 4 shallots

1 small fennel bulb

⅓ pound fresh white or brown
    cultivated mushrooms

2 tablespoons butter

¼ cup minced fresh parsley

¼ cup Lemon-Infused Olive Oil
    (page 38)

4 tablespoons fresh Meyer lemon juice,
    or 4 tablespoons other lemon juice
    mixed with 1 teaspoon sugar

½ teaspoon salt

½ teaspoon freshly ground black pepper

add the fennel and sauté for another 2 to 3 minutes. Finally, add the mushrooms and sauté until they are just tender but not mushy, 3 to 4 minutes. Remove from the heat and stir in the parsley. Fill each artichoke center with an equal amount of the fennel mixture; the amount will depend upon the size of the artichoke. Place the filled artichokes stem end down in a shallow baking dish, just large enough to hold them snugly.

In a small bowl, whisk together the olive oil, 2 tablespoons of the lemon juice, the salt, and pepper until well blended. Pour about one-third of this mixture into the bottom of the baking dish and then pour the remainder over the tops of the artichokes. Cover lightly with aluminum foil to protect the tender outer leaves. Place in the oven and bake for 10 to 15 minutes to heat through and let the flavors blend. Remove from the oven and let stand for 15 minutes. Drizzle each artichoke with a little of the remaining 2 tablespoons lemon juice.

Serve the artichokes warm or at room temperature with the dish juices spooned over them.

TOMATO FLAN WITH SAUCE VERTE

SERVES 4 TO 6

A FLAN IS ESSENTIALLY A CUSTARD MADE WITH MILK OR CREAM AND EGGS. IN FRENCH KITCHENS, SAVORY VERSIONS MADE WITH VEGETABLES, CHEESES, MEATS, HERBS, AND SPICES ARE AS COMMON AS ARE SWEET FLANS. ◎ THIS FIRST-COURSE FLAN, REPLETE WITH SUMMER'S FLAVORS OF TOMATO AND BASIL, IS SERVED CHILLED. WITH BREAD AND SALAD ALONGSIDE, IT MAKES A LIGHT AND REFRESHING SUMMER LUNCH.

Preheat an oven to 325 degrees F.

Peel the tomatoes by plunging them into boiling water for a second or two to loosen the skins, or by peeling them with a small knife as you would a potato. Halve the tomatoes and remove the seeds, then place them in a food processor fitted with the metal blade or in a blender. Purée them and set aside.

In a small skillet over medium heat, melt 1 ½ tablespoons of the butter. Add the onion and sauté until translucent, 3 to 4 minutes. Remove from heat and cool.

In a large bowl, beat together the eggs and cream until well blended. Add the puréed tomatoes, cooled onion, salt, and thyme and mix well.

Grease a straight-sided flan, quiche, or cake pan 8 inches in diameter with the remaining ½ tablespoon butter. Pour the tomato-egg mixture into the prepared pan and then set the filled pan inside a larger one. Pour hot water into the larger pan until it reaches one-half to three-fourths of the way up the sides of the flan-filled pan.

Carefully place the pans on the center rack of the oven and bake until a wooden toothpick inserted into the center of the flan comes out clean, 1 to 1 ¼ hours.

Remove the pans from the oven and then gently lift the flan pan out of the larger pan. Let the flan cool at room temperature for 1 hour, then cover and refrigerate for at least 1 hour or for up to 6 hours before serving.

To unmold the flan for serving, slip a knife all along the inside edge of the mold to loosen the custard from the edges. Invert a serving platter on top of the flan mold and, holding the platter and mold firmly together, flip them over. Gently lift off the mold. Garnish the serving platter with basil sprigs. Cover the top of the flan with a thin layer of the *Sauce Verte.* Cut into wedges to serve.

3 pounds ripe tomatoes (about 10 medium-sized)

2 tablespoons butter

1 yellow onion, minced

5 eggs

½ cup heavy cream

½ teaspoon salt

½ teaspoon minced fresh thyme

Fresh basil sprigs for garnish

½ cup Sauce Verte (page 30)

BRUSSELS SPROUTS POACHED IN CIDER
WITH ONIONS AND APPLES

SERVES 4 TO 6

FOR ME, THIS DISH CONJURES UP THE NORMAN COUNTRYSIDE IN LATE AUTUMN AND EARLY WINTER WHEN THE LAST FALL APPLES ARE STILL ON THE GROUND BENEATH THE TREES, BUT THE FIRST CIDER HAS ALREADY BEEN PRESSED. THE ROLLING HILLS HAVE MIST HANGING ABOUT THEM UNTIL LATE INTO THE MORNING AND YOU SENSE, AS YOU DRIVE ALONG, THAT IF YOU HAVE THE GOOD FORTUNE TO BE INVITED INTO THE KITCHEN OF ONE OF THE STONE FARMHOUSES THAT DOT THE COUNTRYSIDE, YOU WILL SURELY BE OFFERED A SMALL GLASS OF WARMING HOMEMADE CALVADOS.

1 pound brussels sprouts

2 Golden Delicious or other sweet apples

2 tablespoons butter

2 tablespoons olive oil

1 yellow or red onion, chopped

1 ½ cups apple cider

½ teaspoon salt

½ teaspoon freshly ground black pepper

2 star anise

¼ cup balsamic vinegar

Trim the stems from the sprouts and cut each sprout in half from the top through the stem end. Halve and core the apples, peel them if you wish, and cut them into ½-inch cubes.

In a skillet or heavy-bottomed saucepan large enough to hold all the ingredients eventually, melt the butter with the olive oil over low heat. When they begin to foam, increase the heat to medium and add the onions and apples. Sauté until the apples have softened and the onions are translucent, 3 to 4 minutes. Add the sprouts and sauté, stirring gently, for 3 or 4 minutes. Add the apple cider, salt, pepper, and star anise. Cover and reduce the heat to low. Simmer until the sprouts are easily pierced with a fork, 10 to 15 minutes.

Using a slotted spoon, remove the contents of the pan to a warmed serving dish, discard the star anise and cover to keep warm. Increase the heat to medium-high and cook until the pan juices are reduced by half. Add the vinegar and cook for 2 to 3 minutes longer, stirring and scraping the pan to loosen any bits that may be stuck to it.

Pour the hot pan juices over the sprouts mixture and serve immediately.

SALAD OF FRESH SHELL AND SNAP BEANS WITH WINTER SAVORY

SERVES 4 TO 6

MANY VARIETIES OF SHELL BEANS HAVE DISTINCT TASTES AND CHARACTERISTICS. WHEN THEY ARE COMBINED, AS IN THIS SALAD, WITH SEVERAL TYPES OF EDIBLE PODDED BEANS, WHICH ALSO DISPLAY INDIVIDUAL TASTES AND TEXTURES, YOU WILL DISCOVER A SPRIGHTLY MEDLEY OF FLAVORS ONE DOESN'T USUALLY ASSOCIATE WITH BEANS. SERVED WITH A SPOONFUL OR TWO OF FRESHLY CHOPPED TOMATOES LIGHTLY SAUTÉED IN BUTTER AND ONIONS, AND ACCOMPANIED WITH CROUTONS, THIS DISH IS A MEMORABLE FIRST COURSE.

1 pound assorted young, tender snap beans, such as yellow wax, French haricot vert, tiny Blue Lake, and Burgundy purple pod, in any combination

2 pounds assorted fresh shell beans, such as cranberry, black-eyed pea, flageolet, lima, and fava, in any combination

1 clove garlic, minced

2 shallots, minced

½ cup olive oil

⅓ cup red wine vinegar

1 tablespoon minced fresh winter savory

1 tablespoon minced fresh parsley

½ teaspoon salt

1 teaspoon freshly ground black pepper

Trim the tips and remove any strings from the snap beans. Place them on a steamer rack over boiling water, cover, and steam until tender when pierced with the tip of a knife but still brightly colored, about 10 minutes. Immediately remove from the steamer rack and rinse under cold running water to halt the cooking. Drain well and set aside.

Remove the shell beans from their pods, discarding the pods. Place the beans on the steamer rack over boiling water, cover, and steam until tender and all hint of crunchiness is gone. The cooking time may be as little as 10 minutes or as long as 30 minutes or longer, depending upon the size and maturity of the beans. Remove from the steamer and rinse under cold running water to halt the cooking. Drain well and set aside.

To make the dressing, in a large glass or ceramic bowl, whisk together the garlic, shallots, olive oil, vinegar, savory, parsley, salt, and pepper until well blended. Add the snap beans and the shell beans and toss to mix well. Cover and refrigerate for at least 3 hours or as long as overnight.

Serve the salad chilled or at room temperature.

SAUTÉ OF BABY SPINACH

SERVES 3 OR 4

GARDEN-CLIPPED SPINACH LEAVES, NO LARGER THAN A SILVER DOLLAR, TAKE ONLY SECONDS TO SAUTÉ TO A BRIGHT GREEN FINISH. A SQUEEZE OF LEMON JUICE IS ADDED JUST BEFORE THE SPINACH ARRIVES SIZZLING HOT AT THE TABLE. EACH MOUTHFUL EXPLODES IN A BOUQUET OF PURE, SIMPLE FLAVORS. SERVE WITH TOASTY CROUTONS, PERHAPS SPREAD WITH **TAPENADE** (PAGE 32), BEFORE A PASTA OR A HEARTY BEAN DISH SUCH AS DEEP-DISH **CASSOULET** OF FLAGEOLET BEANS (PAGE 124). IT CAN ALSO BE OFFERED AS AN ACCOMPANIMENT TO A MAIN DISH, SUCH AS MIXED GRILL OF WINTER VEGETABLES WITH DRIED-TOMATO **ÄIOLI** (PAGE 107).

1 tablespoon butter

2 tablespoons olive oil

2 cloves garlic, minced

6 cups baby spinach leaves

Juice of 1 lemon

In a large skillet over medium heat, melt the butter with the olive oil. When they begin to foam, add the garlic and spinach leaves. Cover and cook for about 1 minute. Uncover, stir the spinach a bit, and cover again. Cook until the spinach has barely wilted but is still bright green, another 30 seconds to 1 minute.

Remove from the heat, stir in the lemon juice, and serve immediately.

EGGPLANT AND ZUCCHINI FRITTERS

MY NEIGHBOR IN PROVENCE MAKES PLATTERFULS OF THESE **BEIGNETS** WHENEVER CHILDREN ARE AROUND. THEY GOBBLE THEM UP AS IF THEY WERE DONUTS. SHE MAKES BOTH A SWEET AND SAVORY VERSION, ONE SPRINKLED WITH CONFECTIONERS' SUGAR AND THE OTHER WITH SALT AND PEPPER. (IF SERVING THEM AS A SWEET, DUST WITH THE SUGAR JUST BEFORE SERVING.) THE LATTER MAKES A PERFECT COMPLEMENT TO A SUMMERTIME FEAST OF **RATATOUILLE** (PAGE 104).

¼ cup butter, melted

½ cup milk

1 egg, well beaten

½ teaspoon salt, plus salt to taste

½ cup sifted all-purpose flour

1 small eggplant, unpeeled, cut crosswise
    into slices ¼ inch thick

2 medium-sized zucchini or other
    summer squash, cut crosswise
    into slices ¼ inch thick

Vegetable oil, such as canola or
    sunflower, for frying

Freshly ground black pepper

In a large bowl, combine the melted butter, milk, egg, and the ½ teaspoon salt. Beat for 2 or 3 minutes with an electric or hand-held beater. Beat in the flour, a little at a time, until it has all been incorporated. Slip the vegetable slices into the batter.

In a deep skillet over medium-high heat, pour in the vegetable oil to a depth of 2 inches. When a tiny bit of batter dropped into the oil forms a ball and sizzles, the oil is ready. Working in batches, lift out the batter-coated vegetables with tongs and slip them into the skillet; do not crowd the pan. Reduce the heat to medium and fry, turning once, until the batter puffs and turns golden, about 45 seconds or so on each side. Using tongs, remove the cooked vegetables to paper towels to drain. Repeat, working quickly, until all the vegetables are fried, increasing the heat under the oil if necessary for the batter to puff properly.

Sprinkle the fritters with salt and pepper and serve hot or at room temperature.

FRISÉE SALAD WITH WARM GOAT CHEESE

SERVES 4

THIS IS A CLASSIC BISTRO SALAD THROUGHOUT FRANCE, ALTHOUGH THE TYPE OF CHEESE MAY VARY FROM REGION TO REGION. IN THE NORTH, THE SMALL, THICK **CROTTIN DE CHEVIGNY** DOMINATES, BUT IN THE RURAL VILLAGES IN THE SOUTH, THE CHEESE IS MORE LIKELY TO BE A FRESH ONE. I PREFER TO USE THE FRESH TYPE, FLATTENING THE SLICES INTO PATTIES AND THEN PRESSING THEM INTO HERBED BREAD CRUMBS BEFORE SAUTÉING IN BUTTER. ◉ THE HEADS OF FRISÉE SOLD IN FRANCE ARE EIGHTEEN INCHES OR SO IN DIAMETER AND ALL BUT THE FRINGES OF THE OUTERMOST LEAVES ARE BLANCHED TO A CREAMY PALE YELLOW. THE BLANCHING IS DONE IN THE FIELD A WEEK OR MORE BEFORE HARVEST, EITHER BY GATHERING THE WHOLE HEAD INTO A BUNDLE AND PUTTING A RUBBER BAND AROUND IT OR BY COVERING THE HEARTS WITH PLASTIC CAPS OR CLOCHES. BOTH METHODS SHIELD THE INNER LEAVES FROM THE SUNLIGHT THAT THEY USE TO CREATE GREEN-PIGMENTED CHLOROPHYLL. THE BLANCHED LEAVES ARE MUCH SWEETER AND MILDER THAN GREEN ONES, SO IT IS THESE THAT ARE USED FOR SALADS. ◉ SERVE THE SALAD WITH SLICES OF CRUSTY FRENCH BREAD.

Put the frisée in a large bowl. Drizzle with the vinaigrette and then toss to coat the leaves evenly. Divide the dressed frisée evenly among 4 salad plates and set aside.

Divide the goat cheese into 4 equal portions and shape each portion into a patty about 3 inches in diameter and ½ inch thick. In a bowl, stir together the bread crumbs, thyme, winter savory, salt, and pepper until well mixed. Spread the mixture onto a large plate or a sheet of waxed paper. Place the cheese patties on the herbed bread crumbs and gently press the patties so the crumbs adhere. Turn the patties over and coat the other side in the same way.

In a skillet large enough to hold the cheese patties in a single layer, melt the butter with the olive oil over medium heat. When they begin to foam, reduce the heat to medium-low and place the patties in the pan. Cook until lightly golden on the first side, about 30 seconds. Then turn over the patties and cook until lightly golden on the second side and the cheese has softened, another 30 seconds.

Remove from the heat and place a patty on each salad plate. Serve immediately.

4 cups torn pale yellow frisée leaves

1 cup Shallot Vinaigrette (page 24)

6 ounces fresh goat cheese

3 slices day-old baguette or other sturdy bread, crushed to make fine crumbs

1 tablespoon minced fresh thyme

1 tablespoon minced fresh winter savory

½ teaspoon salt

½ teaspoon freshly ground black pepper

1 tablespoon butter

1 tablespoon olive oil

WARM PEARS, BITTER GREENS, AND BLUE CHEESE

THE PAN JUICES FROM THE WARMED PEARS ARE DEGLAZED WITH BALSAMIC VINEGAR, THEN COMBINED WITH OLIVE OIL TO MAKE THE DRESSING FOR THIS WINTER SALAD. ALTHOUGH I SUGGEST BLUE CHEESE—A BLEU D'AUVERGNE, STILTON, OR GORGONZOLA, FOR EXAMPLE—A SOFT BRIE OR PONT L'EVÊQUE WOULD ALSO BE GOOD. YOU CAN ALSO SUBSTITUTE A MIXTURE OF WATERCRESS AND BELGIAN ENDIVE FOR THE ASSORTED BABY GREENS.

2 cups assorted baby greens, including arugula, frisée, escarole, green chicories, radicchio, and red and green lettuces

¼ pound sharp blue cheese, cut into 4 equal pieces

2 medium-sized pears, preferably a firm winter variety such as Bosc or Anjou

2 tablespoons unsalted butter

½ cup balsamic vinegar

¼ cup olive oil

Divide the greens and cheese among 4 salad plates, arranging them attractively. Set aside.

Halve the pears lengthwise and remove the stems and cores. In a skillet just large enough to hold the 4 pear halves in a single layer, melt the butter over medium heat. When it begins to foam, add the pear halves, placing them cut side down. Cook for 1 or 2 minutes, shaking the pan back and forth to prevent them from sticking. Turn over the pears and cook for 1 minute longer. Remove from the heat and, using a sharp knife, cut each pear half lengthwise into thin slices. Arrange a sliced pear half on each salad plate.

Return the skillet to medium heat and add the vinegar. Cook 1 or 2 minutes, stirring constantly to deglaze. Remove from the heat and stir in the olive oil. Drizzle each pear half with a little of the vinegar-oil mixture and serve immediately.

APPLE AND CELERY ROOT SALAD
WITH HAZELNUTS

SERVES 6 TO 8

I HAD A VERSION OF THIS IN THE DINING ROOM OF A SMALL PROVINCIAL HOTEL IN NORMANDY ON AN AGRICULTURAL MARKET DAY. IT WAS A SCENE STRAIGHT FROM A ZOLA NOVEL. THE VILLAGE SQUARE OUTSIDE STILL HAD STRINGS OF CALVES AND PENS OF HOGS, BUT THE TRADING DAY WAS LARGELY OVER AND THE ACTION HAD MOVED INSIDE. THE DINING ROOM WAS POPULATED WITH THE LOCAL AND VISITING GENTRY, DRESSED FOR THE MOST PART IN VINTAGE BUSINESS SUITS. FEW WOMEN WERE DINING. THE ADJOINING BAR, ITS WINDOWS STEAMED, WAS PACKED WITH FARMERS IN HEAVY SWEATERS AND WOOLEN PANTS, LAUGHING AND JOKING AT THE COUNTER OR ENGAGED IN SERIOUS CONVERSATION AT CORNER TABLES. ❦ THERE WERE NO CHOICES ON THE MENU—JUST THIS WONDERFUL SALAD FULL OF THE FLAVOR OF THE **TERROIR**, HEAPED ON A BED OF BELGIAN ENDIVE, FOLLOWED BY A MAIN COURSE AND POMMES PURÉE, AND AN APPLE TART. THE SALAD ALSO MAKES A SATISFYING MAIN COURSE FOR FOUR.

5 apples, such as Gala, Red Delicious,
   or Winesap
6 tablespoons fresh lemon juice
2 medium-sized celery roots, peeled
8 celery stalks (about ¾ bunch)
½ cup mayonnaise
⅓ cup plain yogurt
1 ½ tablespoons Dijon-style mustard
1 teaspoon salt
1 teaspoon freshly ground black pepper
¼ teaspoon crushed dill seeds
12 to 16 Belgian endive leaves
   (2 or 3 heads)
⅓ cup chopped hazelnuts

Halve and core the apples but do not peel. Cut them into small cubes and place in a large bowl. Sprinkle with 3 tablespoons of the lemon juice and toss to coat. Shred the celery root on the large holes of a hand-held grater. Dice the celery into ¼-inch pieces. Add the celery root and celery to the apples and toss again.

In a small bowl, combine the mayonnaise, yogurt, mustard, the remaining 3 tablespoons lemon juice, the salt, pepper, and dill seeds. Stir to mix well. Add the dressing to the apple mixture and toss thoroughly. Taste and adjust the seasonings, if necessary.

Arrange the Belgian endive leaves on individual salad plates, dividing them equally. Top with the salad and garnish with the hazelnuts. Serve at once.

TELEME CHEESE AND SAUTÉED
GREEN ONION CROQUE

SERVES 1

CREAMY TELEME THOROUGHLY LACED WITH SAUTÉED GREEN ONION OOZES OUT ALL THE SIDES OF THIS TASTY VERSION OF THE FAMED EGG BATTER–FRIED SANDWICH. GRILLED OR SAUTÉED LEEKS, SWEET OR HOT PEPPERS, OR CHOPPED ARTICHOKE HEARTS CAN BE USED INSTEAD OF GREEN ONIONS TO OFFER VARIATIONS IN COLOR, TASTE, AND TEXTURE. OTHER SOFT CHEESES SUCH AS BEL PAESE OR CAMEMBERT CAN BE USED, TOO. ◉ MULTIPLY THE INGREDIENTS TO SERVE AS MANY PEOPLE AS YOU LIKE. ACCOMPANY WITH SALAD OF FRESH SHELL BEANS AND SNAP BEANS WITH WINTER SAVORY (PAGE 66), A BOWL OF FRESH PEA SOUP WITH **CRÈME FRAÎCHE** AND CHIVE BLOSSOMS (PAGE 49), OR PROVENÇAL TOMA-TOES (PAGE 58), FOLLOWED BY FRUIT OR HOMEMADE ICE CREAM.

In a small cup, stir together the mayonnaise and mustard and then spread it on one side of each of the bread slices. Set aside.

In a skillet over medium heat, warm 2 tablespoons of the olive oil. Add the green onions and sauté until translucent, 2 to 3 minutes. Remove from the heat and sprinkle with the salt.

Spread the onions across 1 slice of the mayonnaise-mustard–spread bread. Top with the cheese. Place the other slice of bread, mayonnaise-mustard side face down, on the top. Press together.

In a shallow bowl, lightly beat the egg. In a clean skillet just large enough to hold the sandwich, heat the remaining olive oil and the butter over medium heat. Drench both sides of the sandwich in the beaten egg and slip the sandwich into the skillet. Fry until the first side is golden, 3 or 4 minutes. Turn over the sand-wich and fry on the second side until golden, 2 or 3 minutes longer.

Transfer to a plate and serve at once.

1 tablespoon mayonnaise

1 tablespoon Dijon-style mustard

2 slices sturdy bread, such as a pumper-nickel or country French

3 tablespoons olive oil

6 green onions, including the tender green tops, chopped

⅛ teaspoon salt

1 slice Teleme or other soft cheese (about 2 ounces)

1 egg

1 tablespoon butter

WARM FENNEL IN VINAIGRETTE

SERVES 4 TO 6

DRESSING A WARM STEAMED OR BRAISED VEGETABLE WITH VINAIGRETTE IS A WONDERFUL WAY TO BRING OUT ITS FLAVOR. FENNEL IS USED HERE, BUT LEEKS, CELERY HEARTS, BELGIAN ENDIVES, ASPARAGUS, BEETS, OR POTATOES ARE ALL GOOD CANDIDATES FOR THIS PRESENTATION. A GARNISH OF GRATED OR CRUMBLED CHEESE, FINELY DICED HARD-COOKED EGGS, AND HERBS SUCH AS TARRAGON, CHERVIL, CHIVES, OR PARSLEY WILL ADD YET ANOTHER SUBTLE LAYER OF FLAVOR TO THIS CLASSIC PREPARATION.

Trim the fennel bulbs, discarding any tough or discolored outer leaves and cutting away any stalks and feathery tops. Cut the bulbs, from the top through the stem end, into ¼-inch-thick slices. Arrange the slices on a steamer rack over boiling water, cover, and steam until tender when pierced with the tines of a fork, about 10 minutes. Remove the fennel slices to a bowl.

Pour the dressing over the warm fennel, gently turning all the slices to make sure they are all evenly coated. Cover and let stand for 15 to 30 minutes before serving.

Top with the cheese and chervil and serve warm or at room temperature.

4 medium-sized fennel bulbs

¾ cup Mustard Vinaigrette (page 24) or Shallot Vinaigrette (page 24)

1 ounce Asaigo or other hard, aged cheese, shaved into paper-thin slices with a knife or vegetable peeler

1 teaspoon minced fresh chervil

FIG AND ARUGULA SALAD

SERVES 4

ICAN FEAST ON A PLATTER OF THIS SALAD AND ASK NOTHING MORE OF A MEAL. THE COMBINATION OF FIGS, ARUGULA, AND CHEESE BALANCES THE SALTY AND THE SWEET, THE CREAMY AND THE CRUNCHY.

8 ripe fresh figs

¼ pound Roquefort cheese, cut into
   8 equal pieces

25 to 30 young arugula leaves

½ teaspoon freshly ground black pepper

4 to 6 tablespoons olive oil

Cut each fig three-fourths of the way through, from stem to blossom end. Arrange them on a platter or on 4 salad plates, fanning them open slightly. Tuck a piece of cheese into each open fig. Scatter the arugula leaves around the figs. Sprinkle the figs and arugula with the pepper and drizzle each fig with a little olive oil. Serve at once.

CELERY ROOT SALAD WITH LEMON AND CUMIN DRESSING

SERVES 4

CELERY ROOT, A MUCH-USED VEGETABLE THROUGHOUT FRANCE, IS VALUED BY COOKS FOR ITS VERSATILITY AND CRISP, PUNGENT FLAVOR. PROBABLY BEST KNOWN IN THE GUISE OF **CÉLERI-RAVE RÉMOULADE**, THE BISTRO CLASSIC IN WHICH IT IS COATED WITH A SAUCE OF MUSTARD AND MAYONNAISE, CELERY ROOT CAN ALSO BE STEAMED, BRAISED, BROILED, AND, OF COURSE, PREPARED RAW IN ANY NUMBER OF WAYS. HERE, IT IS GIVEN A TREATMENT THAT UTILIZES BRILLIANTLY COLORED TURMERIC AND PUNGENT CUMIN, SPICES ONE FINDS SOLD IN BULK IN OPEN MARKETS THROUGHOUT FRANCE.

½ cup fresh lemon juice

1 teaspoon ground cumin

⅛ teaspoon ground turmeric

⅛ teaspoon salt

¼ teaspoon freshly ground black pepper

2 tablespoons minced fresh parsley

1 large celery root (about 1 pound), peeled

In a medium-sized bowl, whisk together the lemon juice, cumin, turmeric, salt, pepper, and parsley. Set aside.

Finely julienne the celery root on a mandoline or with a sharp knife. The slices should be no more than $\frac{1}{16}$ inch thick, if possible.

Add the celery root to the lemon juice mixture and toss to coat well. Serve at once.

WILD ASPARAGUS AND SCRAMBLED EGGS

SERVES 4

EVERY SPRING, WILD ASPARAGUS FLOURISH ON THE HILLSIDES OF PROVENCE. THE INTENSELY FLAVORED THIN STALKS REQUIRE ONLY THE BRIEFEST OF COOKING. TRADITIONALLY, THEY ARE ADDED TO FARM-FRESH SCRAMBLED EGGS, AND SERVED AS A SPECIAL SPRINGTIME FIRST COURSE AT EITHER LUNCH OR DINNER. I FIND THAT WHEN THIN ASPARAGUS ARE AVAILABLE IN OUR MARKETS OR FROM OUR HOME GARDENS, THEY ARE A GOOD SUBSTITUTE FOR THE WILD ONES.

Trim the asparagus, discarding any woody or tough ends. Cut the spears into ½-inch-long pieces. Place the pieces on a steamer rack over boiling water, cover, and steam until they are still bright green but tender when pierced with the tip of a knife, about 20 seconds. Rinse the asparagus under cold running water to halt the cooking, drain well, and set aside.

In a skillet over medium heat, melt the butter. When it begins to foam, reduce the heat to medium-low and add the eggs. Scramble them until just barely firm, 2 or 3 minutes. Stir in the asparagus, salt, pepper, and *crème fraîche*, mixing gently. Reduce the heat to low and cook for another minute.

Spoon onto individual warmed plates and serve immediately.

½ pound asparagus, preferably thin

3 tablespoons butter

10 eggs, beaten

½ teaspoon salt

1 teaspoon freshly ground black pepper

¼ cup crème fraîche

PARSNIP AND MUSHROOM FLAN

SERVES 4 TO 6

BEFORE THE POTATO ARRIVED FROM THE NEW WORLD, THE PARSNIP WAS THE PRIMARY STARCH VEGETABLE OF NORTHERN EUROPE. IT, LIKE ITS USURPER, WAS BAKED, BOILED, ROASTED, BUT-TERED, MASHED, AND PUT INTO STEWS, SOUPS, AND PIES. HERE, IN A VARIATION ON THE CLASSIC POTATO AND HAM FLAN, THE PARSNIP TAKES THE PLACE OF THE POTATO AND THE MUSHROOM ASSUMES THE ROLE OF THE HAM. A WEDGE OF THIS FLAN IS PARTICULARLY GOOD ACCOMPANIED WITH A LITTLE SALAD OF MIXED YOUNG GREENS SERVED ON THE SAME PLATE.

4 tablespoons butter

½ cup minced yellow onion

*½ cup minced fresh mushroom, such
   as portobello or chanterelle*

3 eggs

1 cup heavy cream

½ cup milk

1 teaspoon salt

1 teaspoon freshly ground black pepper

¼ cup minced fresh parsley

*1 ½ cups peeled and grated parsnip
   (3 or 4 parsnips)*

Preheat an oven to 375 degrees F.

Thoroughly grease a 10-inch pie dish with 1 tablespoon of the butter. In a small skillet, melt the remaining 3 tablespoons of butter over medium heat. When it begins to foam, add the onion and mushroom and sauté, stirring often, until the onion is translucent, 3 to 4 minutes. Remove from the heat and set aside to cool.

In a large bowl, using a fork or whisk, beat together the eggs, cream, and milk until well blended. Add the salt, pepper, parsley, the onion-mushroom mixture, and the grated parsnip. Mix well. Pour the contents of the bowl into the pre-pared pie dish.

Bake until the top is puffed and golden and a knife inserted into the center comes out clean, about 30 minutes. Remove from the oven and serve immediately or let cool slightly. Cut into wedges and place on individual plates.

ROASTED GARLIC

SERVES 4

WHEN GARLIC IS COOKED, IT LOSES MUCH OF ITS STRONG TASTE BUT RETAINS ITS FLAVOR. WHEN ROASTED, IT BECOMES DELICIOUSLY CREAMY AND SLIGHTLY CARAMELIZED. FRESH NEW CROP GARLIC WHICH ARRIVES IN JULY IS BEST FOR ROASTING, AS THE CLOVES ARE STILL FIRM AND THE FLAVOR TRUE. THE ROASTED CLOVES HAVE A NUMBER OF DIFFERENT USES; THEY CAN BE PURÉED AND USED AS A SPREAD, ADDED TO A **BÉCHAMEL** OR OTHER SAUCE, BLENDED INTO SOUPS AND STEWS, OR WHIPPED INTO FLUFFY PURÉED POTATOES. WHOLE CLOVES CAN BE FOLDED INTO PASTAS OR ADDED TO WARM SALADS, SOUPS, OR STEWS. ❁ MY FAVORITE USE IS TO SERVE A WHOLE HEAD OF ROASTED GARLIC PER PERSON, ALONG WITH A FRESH CREAMY GOAT CHEESE, A BASKET OF THICK BAGUETTE SLICES OR ANOTHER STURDY BREAD, AND A BIG BOWL OF WELL-SEASONED SALAD. A HANDS-ON DISH, THE CLOVES ARE PULLED APART AND THEN SQUEEZED, RELEASING THEIR CREAMY INTERIOR ONTO THE BREAD FOR SPREADING ALONG WITH A BIT OF CHEESE. SERVED THUS, IT IS ENOUGH FOR A LIGHT LUNCH, A FIRST COURSE, OR AS AN ACCOMPANIMENT TO A MAIN DISH.

Preheat an oven to 300 degrees F.

Using a sharp knife, cut off the tops of the whole garlic heads. Do not remove the papery skin. Rub each head with 1 tablespoon of the olive oil, ½ teaspoon of the salt, ½ teaspoon of the pepper, and 1 tablespoon of the fresh thyme. Place the heads upright in a shallow baking dish just large enough to hold them. Dot each head with ½ tablespoon of the butter.

Roast uncovered for 20 minutes. Cover loosely with aluminum foil and bake until the cloves are soft and easily pierced with the tip of a sharp knife, 10 to 15 minutes. Remove and let cool until they can be handled easily, about 15 minutes.

Serve whole or, to use the cloves in another preparation, peel away the outer layer of skin from each head. Then carefully squeeze each head from the bottom, "popping" each clove from its skin. Be careful not to squish the cloves. Use as desired.

4 heads garlic, preferably new crop

4 tablespoons olive oil

2 teaspoons salt

2 teaspoons freshly ground black pepper

4 tablespoons minced fresh thyme

2 tablespoons butter

SALAD OF BELGIAN ENDIVE, CRUMBLED PARMESAN, AND WALNUTS

SERVES 4 TO 6

BELGIAN ENDIVE IS ONE OF THE MOST COMMONLY USED WINTER SALAD GREENS, NOT ONLY IN FRANCE BUT THROUGHOUT NORTHERN EUROPE. THE PLUMP, TORPEDO-SHAPED HEADS, OR **CHICONS**, ARE THE RESULT OF A SECOND GROWTH FORCED FROM ROOTS DUG IN SUMMER AND FALL AND THEN STORED AT COLD TEMPERATURES. THE ROOTS ARE BROUGHT FROM THE COLD INTO WARMER TEMPERATURES TO INITIATE, OR FORCE, THE SECOND FLUSH OF LEAVES. THUS, BELGIAN ENDIVE CAN BE "GROWN" THROUGHOUT WINTER WHEN MANY LOCAL GREENS CANNOT. BECAUSE THE **CHICONS** ARE FORCED IN THE DARK, THE LEAVES ARE WHITE, SUCCULENT, AND MILD. HEADS WITH GREEN LEAVES HAVE SUFFERED FROM EXTENDED EXPOSURE TO LIGHT AND THEIR FLAVOR WILL BE BITTER. ❀ BELGIAN ENDIVE IS MOST OFTEN PAIRED WITH OTHER WINTER STORAGE INGREDIENTS, SUCH AS CHEESES, NUTS, DRIED FRUITS, ONIONS, OR THE SEASON'S CITRUS FRUITS, AND MAY BE SERVED AT THE BEGINNING OF THE MEAL OR FOLLOWING THE MAIN COURSE.

4 Belgian endives

½ cup Classic Vinaigrette (page 24)

¼ pound Parmesan or other hard, aged cheese, crumbled

½ cup walnut bits

Prepare the Belgian endives by making a V-shaped cut in the bottom of each one to remove the core. Separate the leaves, cutting the large ones in half lengthwise and leaving the smaller ones intact.

Put the vinaigrette in a large salad bowl. Add the leaves and turn them with a large spoon until they are well coated. Strew with the cheese and all but a few of the walnuts and toss. Garnish with the remaining walnuts and serve at once.

CHAPTER THREE

MAIN COURSES

MAIN COURSES

IT HAS NOT BEEN TOO MANY YEARS SINCE A TYPICAL FRENCH HOUSEHOLD WOULD HAVE NOT ONE BUT TWO MAIN COURSES. Today, however, that is rarely the case, except at the home of my neighbor Françoise, when she invites me over for a meal. Then, we have not only two main courses, but often two separate vegetable courses as well, since she has a large *potager* (a kitchen garden, which I share with her) and her husband's passions are growing vegetables and melons.

Main dishes, like first courses, rely on the seasonal ingredients of the region, but they tend to be more complex in flavor, served in larger portions, and generally more substantial than the preceding course.

Sometimes a main course is a soup—a sturdy, filling *soupe au pistou*, full of the plump, fresh *coco* beans that impart such a distinctive flavor. It may be platter of couscous or another pasta garnished with cauliflower or sweet young peas. Stews, gratins, and terrines are all candidates for main dishes made only of vegetables, and their components reflect and celebrate the season and the *terroir*.

GLACÉ CARROTS, SHALLOTS, AND FENNEL

THE VEGETABLES GRADUALLY ABSORB THE BUTTER AND BROTH IN WHICH THEY ARE SLOWLY COOKED, AND THEIR NATURAL SUGARS ARE ENHANCED BY A LITTLE ADDITIONAL SUGAR. AT THE END OF THE COOKING, THE HEAT IS INCREASED, THE SHERRY-SOAKED BITS OF DATES ARE ADDED, AND THE VEGETABLES ARE TURNED AND COATED, CARAMELIZING ALONG WITH THE SAUCE. THE END RESULT IS DELICIOUSLY RICH. THE VEGETABLES MAY BE SERVED JUST AS THEY ARE, ACCOMPANIED WITH A GREEN SALAD, OR THEY CAN BE PUT INTO A BUTTERED FLAMEPROOF CASSEROLE, TOPPED WITH A HALF RECIPE OF THE CELERY ROOT AND POTATO PURÉE (PAGE 47), DOTTED WITH BUTTER, AND SLIPPED UNDER A BROILER UNTIL THE TOP IS SLIGHTLY BROWNED, 3 TO 4 MINUTES. THIS VERSION WILL SERVE FIVE.

Pour the sherry into a small bowl and add the dates. Set aside.

Bring a saucepan full of water to a boil. Add the shallots and parboil for 5 minutes. Drain, let cool, and then remove the papery skins. Trim off the tips of the root ends, but do not cut into the flesh or the shallots may not stay intact during cooking. Set aside.

Trim the fennel bulbs, discarding any tough or discolored outer leaves and cutting away any stalks and feathery tops. Cut each bulb, from the top through the root stem end, in quarters. Set aside.

In a saucepan or skillet just large enough to hold the vegetables in a crowded single layer, melt the butter over medium heat. When it begins to foam, add the carrots, shallots, and fennel. Sprinkle with the sugar, salt, and pepper. Reduce the heat to low and turn the vegetables in the butter. Cook, continuing to turn until they are well coated and slightly softened, 4 to 5 minutes. Add the broth and let cook, turning often until the shallots and fennel have begun to take on a brownish gold hue and the carrots are tender, 20 to 25 minutes.

Drain the dates, reserving the sherry. Add the dates, 1 teaspoon of the sherry, and the thyme or winter savory. Raise the heat to medium-high and cook until the vegetables are browned and caramelized, another 3 or 4 minutes.

To serve, transfer to a warmed serving dish and serve at once.

¼ cup dry sherry

4 large dried Medjool or other sweet
    dates, pitted and chopped

12 shallots, unpeeled

3 medium-sized fennel bulbs

½ cup (¼ pound) butter

8 fingerling-sized carrots, peeled but left
    whole, or 2 medium-sized carrots,
    peeled and each cut into 4 pieces

2 tablespoons sugar

½ teaspoon salt

1 teaspoon freshly ground black pepper

¾ cup Leek and Mushroom Broth
    (page 20) or other vegetable broth

1 teaspoon minced fresh thyme or
    winter savory

TIAN OF CELERY ROOT, TURNIP, FENNEL, AND RUTABAGA

SERVES 4 TO 6

I SUSPECT THIS, OR SOME VERSION OF IT, MUST HAVE BEEN A POPULAR NINETEENTH-CENTURY DISH EATEN BY THE POOR. NEVERTHELESS, LIKE MANY OTHER SIMPLE DISHES, IT IS WORTHY OF OUR CONSIDERATION. RICH WITH ASSERTIVE TASTES AND TEXTURES—THERE IS NOTHING TIMID ABOUT RUTABAGAS AND TURNIPS—IT MAKES A GOOD MATCH WITH WEDGES OF CREAMY POLENTA AND A PLATTER OF WILTED SPINACH OR MUSTARD GREENS.

⅓ cup all-purpose flour

1 teaspoon salt

1 tablespoon freshly ground black pepper

4 cloves garlic, minced

¼ cup chopped celery root leaves

¼ cup chopped fresh parsley

¼ cup chopped fresh chives

4 tablespoons olive oil

2 medium-sized fennel bulbs

2 medium-sized turnips, peeled and cut
   into 1- to 1½-inch cubes

1 medium-sized rutabaga, peeled and cut
   into 1- to 1½-inch cubes

½ large celery root, peeled and cut into
   1- to 1½-inch cubes

1 cup Basic Vegetable Broth (page 22)
   or other vegeatable broth

Preheat an oven to 325 degrees F.

In a large bowl, combine the flour, salt, pepper, garlic, celery root leaves, parsley, and chives. Set aside.

Using 1½ to 2 tablespoons of the olive oil, thoroughly grease the bottom and sides of a baking dish just large enough to hold the vegetables in a double layer. Trim the fennel bulbs, discarding any tough or discolored outer leaves and cutting away any stalks and feathery tops. Cut each bulb, from the top through the stem end, into 6 wedges. Place the fennel wedges in the prepared dish along with the turnips, rutabaga, and celery root, arranging them in two layers. Drizzle the vegetables with the remaining olive oil. Add ¼ cup of the broth.

Bake until a golden crust has formed and the vegetables beneath are soft and easily pierced with the tines of a fork, about 2 hours, adding the remaining broth ¼ cup at a time as the vegetables absorb it.

Remove from the oven. To serve, scoop out with a serving spoon onto warmed individual plates. Serve at once.

VEGETABLE SOUP
WITH PISTOU

SERVES 15

ONE AUGUST IN PROVENCE, I WENT TO A MIDNIGHT VILLAGE **FÊTE**. THE TOWN WAS PERCHED HIGH ON A HILLSIDE AND MOST OF THE STREETS WERE NARROW, STEEP, AND CURVING. THE ONLY FLAT PLACE WAS A TINY SQUARE IN FRONT OF A CHURCH, AND IT WAS HERE THAT THE LONG TABLES FOR THE **FÊTE** WERE SET. FROM A TINY RESTAURANT OFF THE SQUARE, HUGE BOWLS OF SUMMER VEGETABLE SOUP WERE BROUGHT STEAMING HOT TO THE TABLES, ALONG WITH SMALLER BOWLS OF FRAGRANT **PISTOU** — A SAUCE OF GARLIC, BASIL, AND OLIVE OIL. THE GRATED CHEESE WAS ALREADY ON THE TABLES, ALONG WITH BAGUETTES FROM THE LOCAL **BOULANGERIE** AND BOTTLES OF THE LOCAL ROSÉ AND RED WINE. UNDER THE COVER OF SPREADING MULBERRY TREES STRUNG WITH COLORED LIGHTS, WE SAT OUT TALKING AND EATING, WHILE THE CICADAS SANG IN THE BACKGROUND. ◉ **SOUPE AU PISTOU** IS IDEAL TO SERVE TO A LARGE CROWD, AS THE SOUP IS EASY TO MAKE IN GOOD-SIZED QUANTITIES AND CAN BE PREPARED A DAY AHEAD. BECAUSE THE DISH USES FRESH SHELL BEANS, AVAILABLE ONLY DURING THE SUMMER, IT BRINGS TO THE TABLE THE CACHET OF A SPECIAL MOMENT CAPTURED IN TIME. ◉ DO NOT BE TEMPTED TO MAKE THE **PISTOU** AHEAD OF TIME, HOWEVER. FRESHLY MADE, IT HAS AN INTENSE, SHARP FLAVOR THAT ENHANCES ALL THE OTHER INGREDIENTS IN THE SOUP. LEFT TO STAND, IT CAN BECOME DULL AND EVEN BITTER AND, IF STIRRED DIRECTLY INTO A SOUP THAT WILL BE REHEATED LATER, WILL GIVE THE SOUP AN ENTIRELY DIFFERENT FLAVOR.

To make the soup, chop the tomatoes, reserving the seeds and juices. Set aside. In a soup pot large enough to hold all the ingredients eventually, heat the olive oil over medium heat. Add the onions and the garlic and sauté until translucent, 3 to 4 minutes. Add the potatoes, snap beans, and shell beans, and cook over medium heat, stirring almost constantly with a wooden spoon, until well-coated and slightly softened, 5 to 6 minutes. Stir in the chopped tomatoes and their juices and seeds. Add the broth, salt, pepper, thyme, marjoram, and the cheese rind, if using. Reduce the heat, cover, and simmer, stirring occasionally, until the potatoes and beans are soft, about 40 minutes. Add the pasta and cook until it is tender, 10 to 15 minutes.

Meanwhile, make the *pistou*. Place the garlic cloves in a large bowl and mash them with the back of a wooden spoon or with a pestle. Add the basil leaves,

For the soup:

*4 pounds very ripe tomatoes
(about 12 medium-sized)*

¼ cup olive oil

2 yellow onions, chopped

6 cloves garlic, chopped

*8 medium-sized boiling or new potatoes,
such as Yukon Gold or White or Red
Rose (about 3 pounds), peeled, if
desired, and cut into 1-inch dice*

½ pound Blue Lake or other slender
    green snap beans, trimmed and cut
    into 1-inch lengths
2 cups fresh shell beans, such as fava,
    cranberry, flageolet, or lima (about
    1 pound)
3 quarts Basic Vegetable Broth (page
    22), or other vegetable broth
2 teaspoons salt
2 teaspoons freshly ground black pepper
2 tablespoons fresh thyme leaves
1 teaspoon minced fresh marjoram
1 piece Parmesan or other hard cheese
    rind, 2 to 4 inches square, chopped
    (optional)

For the pistou:
1 cup finely broken spaghetti or
    other thin pasta
10 garlic cloves
4 cups fresh basil leaves
½ cup olive oil
1 teaspoon salt
¼ cup freshly grated Parmesan
    cheese, if needed

1 cup at a time, mashing them into the garlic paste. When all the basil has been incorporated, add the olive oil, a drizzle at a time, incorporating it into the paste along with the salt. If you have not added the cheese rind to the soup, mix the grated Parmesan into the *pistou*.

To serve, ladle the soup into bowls and stir about 1 tablespoon *pistou* into each bowl. Serve the remaining *pistou* in a bowl alongside.

SPRING VEGETABLE RAGOUT

SERVES 4

THE FLAVOR AND TEXTURE OF NEW SPRING VEGETABLES ARE SO DELICATE THAT PREPARING THEM REQUIRES LITTLE MORE THAN BRIEF COOKING IN BUTTER IN A COVERED PAN. GREEN SHALLOTS, WHICH ARE THE FIRST TENDER SHOOTS PUT FORTH BY THE BULBS, ARE ESPECIALLY FLAVORFUL, AS ARE THE TINY YOUNG TURNIPS, CARROTS, AND OTHER EARLY SEASON VEGETABLES. THEY RELEASE SOME OF THEIR JUICES WHEN COOKED, WHICH, IN THIS RECIPE, COMBINE WITH WHITE WINE AND FRESH HERBS TO MAKE A SAUCE.

Shell the fava beans and discard the pods. Then remove the thin peel that coats each bean by slitting the edge with a knife and "popping" the bean out. You should have about 1 cup beans. Set aside.

Cut the turnips and the potatoes in half and set aside. Trim the asparagus, discarding any woody or tough ends. Cut the asparagus on the diagonal into pieces about 2 inches long; set aside. Trim the shallots or green onions and then cut into 2-inch-long pieces, including all but the last inch or so of the green tops. Set the vegetables aside.

In a heavy-bottomed saucepan over medium heat, melt 3 tablespoons of the butter. When it begins to foam, add the carrots and potatoes. Cover, reduce the heat to low, and cook until the vegetables are well coated with butter and slightly softened, 5 to 7 minutes.

Uncover and add the turnips, salt, pepper, and sugar. Re-cover and cook for 3 or 4 minutes. Add the shallots or green onions, re-cover, and cook until the vegetables are slightly softened, 3 or 4 minutes. Add some of the remaining butter if needed to prevent sticking, and then add the fava beans and peas. Cover and cook over low heat for 8 to 10 minutes. All the vegetables should be almost tender.

Uncover, increase the heat to medium, and add the white wine. Deglaze the pan, stirring and scraping up any bits clinging to the pan bottom, and reduce the wine by one-third. Stir in the asparagus, thyme, parsley, and mint, and any remaining butter. Cover, reduce the heat to low, and cook until the asparagus is just tender, 5 to 7 minutes.

Serve the ragout immediately.

1 pound fava beans

2 or 3 golf ball–sized turnips

¾ pound small new potatoes

½ pound asparagus

4 or 5 green shallots, or 8 green onions

4 tablespoons butter

8 fingerling-sized carrots, peeled

½ teaspoon salt

½ teaspoon freshly ground black pepper

½ teaspoon sugar

¾ pound young English peas, shelled

½ cup dry white wine

1 teaspoon minced fresh thyme

1 tablespoon minced fresh parsley

1 teaspoon minced fresh mint

WINTER VEGETABLE RAGOUT WITH CARAMELIZED WHOLE SHALLOTS

SERVES 4 TO 6

THIS SUBSTANTIAL DISH IS FULL OF THE TASTES OF A WINTER GARDEN. THE SHALLOTS, COOKED SEPARATELY AND ADDED JUST BEFORE SERVING, BRING THEIR FINE, SWEET TASTE UNADULTERATED TO THE FINAL DISH. TOPPINGS OF FRESH MINT, DILL, AND TARRAGON, ALONG WITH YOGURT, REFLECT THE INFLUENCES OF NORTH AFRICA IN FRANCE.

Preheat an oven to 350 degrees F.

Bring a saucepan full of water to a boil. Add the shallots and parboil for 5 minutes. Drain, let cool, and then remove the papery skins. Trim off the tips of the root ends, but do not cut into the flesh or the shallots may not stay intact during cooking. Set aside.

Scrub the vegetables, but do not peel them. Cut the thick upper parts of the parsnips into 1½-inch pieces. Leave the thin root end intact. Cut each turnip and rutabaga into quarters, then halve the quarters to make 8 pieces in all. Cut the carrots into 1½-inch lengths.

Remove the white ribs from the chard (reserve for another use). Cut the chard greens into chiffonade strips by stacking them, rolling them up lengthwise into a thin cigar shape, then cutting across into ⅛-inch-wide "threads."

In a large, flameproof casserole over medium heat, melt 2 tablespoons of the butter with the olive oil. When the mixture begins to foam, add the parsnips, turnips, rutabagas, and carrots. Sauté, turning frequently, until well coated and slightly softened, 5 to 6 minutes.

In a small bowl, stir together the flour, salt, pepper, and turmeric. Sprinkle the mixture over the vegetables. Cook, turning the vegetables often, until the flour mixture has begun to brown, 3 or 4 minutes. Add the wine, stir for a minute or two, and then add the broth, water, half of the chard, and all of the raisins. Cover, place in the oven, and bake until the vegetables are tender when pierced with the tines of a fork, about 45 minutes.

While the vegetables are baking, finish preparing the shallots. Heat the remaining 1 tablespoon butter in a skillet over medium heat. Add the shallots and

12 large shallots, unpeeled

4 parsnips (about 1½ pounds total weight)

2 turnips (about 1 pound total weight)

2 rutabagas (about 1 pound total weight)

2 carrots (about 1 pound total weight)

4 or 5 large green chard leaves

3 tablespoons butter

1 tablespoon olive oil

2 tablespoons all-purpose flour

½ teaspoon salt

½ teaspoon freshly ground black pepper

1 teaspoon ground turmeric

⅓ cup dry white wine

2 cups Leek and Mushroom Broth (page 20) or other vegetable broth

1 cup water

¼ cup raisins

¼ cup chopped fresh dill

¼ cup chopped fresh tarragon

¼ cup chopped fresh mint

¼ cup chopped fresh chives

1 cup plain yogurt

increase the heat to medium-high. Cook the shallots, stirring and turning constantly, 3 to 4 minutes. The shallots will begin to brown and caramelize slightly yet still retain their shape.

To finish the ragout, remove the casserole from the oven and stir in the cooked shallots and the remaining chard. In a small bowl, stir together the dill, tarragon, mint, and chives. Spoon the ragout into shallow bowls or plates and top each portion with several spoonfuls of yogurt and a generous spoonful of mixed herbs. Serve immediately.

SAVOY CABBAGE STUFFED WITH DRIED FRUITS, MUSHROOMS, AND RICE

SERVES 10 TO 12

THIS IS A SHOWSTOPPING DISH THAT IS EVEN BETTER THE SECOND DAY THAN THE FIRST. THE CABBAGE IS PARBOILED, AND THEN THE SOFTENED OUTER LEAVES ARE UNWRAPPED, ONE BY ONE, UNTIL THE SOLID HEART IS REACHED. THE HEART IS REMOVED, TO BE INCORPORATED INTO A SAVORY STUFFING THAT THEN FILLS THE CAVITY TO THE BRIM. THE OUTER LEAVES ARE WRAPPED BACK INTO POSITION, THE WHOLE HEAD IS ENCIRCLED IN CHEESECLOTH, AND THEN IT IS GENTLY COOKED IN A FLAVORFUL BROTH. BROUGHT TO THE TABLE WHOLE, THEN CUT INTO WEDGES FOR SERVING, THIS DISH ELEVATES THE HUMBLE CABBAGE TO CENTERPIECE STATUS. FOLLOW IT WITH WARM PEARS, BITTER GREENS, AND BLUE CHEESE (PAGE 72), AND CONCLUDE WITH A CHOCOLATE CAKE OR MOUSSE AND YOU WILL HAVE PUT TOGETHER A VERY PLEASING MENU.

If the cabbage is from the garden or a farmer's market, it will likely have thick outer leaves. Trim off this tough protective layer of leaves and discard. If using a store-bought cabbage, remove any bruised or discolored outer leaves. Place the cabbage in a large soup pot or stockpot and pour in water to reach halfway up the sides of the cabbage. Add the 2 tablespoons salt, cover, and bring to a boil. Once the water has reached a boil, reduce the heat to medium and continue to cook, covered, for 15 minutes. Meanwhile, line a bowl large enough to hold the cabbage with a 2-foot-square piece of cheesecloth, allowing the excess to drape over the edge.

When the cabbage is done, lift it out of the pot, draining well, and put it in the cheesecloth-lined bowl. Let it stand until cool enough to handle, about 15 minutes. Gently unwrap the leaves, one by one, until you reach the tightly wrapped core of the cabbage, which will be just a little larger than a fist. Using a sharp knife, cut through the core to its base, being careful not to tear the leaves you unwrapped. It may take several cuts to succeed. Remove the center and set aside. Cut away any excess core you may have missed to make a substantial cavity. Set the cabbage aside in the cheesecloth-lined bowl and prepare the filling.

Finely chop the removed center of the cabbage; you should have about 6 cups. In a large skillet over medium heat, melt the butter. When it begins to foam, add

1 large Savoy or other green cabbage (6 to 7 pounds)

2 tablespoons plus 2 teaspoons salt

4 tablespoons butter

½ medium yellow onion, minced

10 dried prunes, pitted and chopped

¼ cup raisins

4 dried apricots, chopped

¾ pound mixed chanterelle and oyster mushrooms or other flavorful mushrooms, chopped

2 teaspoons freshly ground black pepper

½ teaspoon ground cumin

1½ cups broth-cooked long-grained white rice

¼ cup heavy cream

the onion and sauté until translucent, 2 to 3 minutes. Add the prunes, raisins, apricots, and the chopped cabbage. Reduce the heat to medium-low, cover, and cook until the cabbage has thoroughly wilted, having reduced its volume by half, 6 to 8 minutes. Uncover and stir in the mushrooms. Increase the heat to medium and sauté for 3 or 4 minutes. The mushrooms should be softened but not mushy. Stir in the remaining 2 teaspoons salt, the pepper, and cumin. Remove from the heat and transfer the mixture to a large bowl. Add the cooked rice and the cream, stirring and compacting the mixture until it feels like a soft paste.

Fill the cavity of the cabbage with the mixture, rounding it a bit over the brim. Starting from the innermost leaf, rewrap the cabbage. When the last leaf is folded over, gather up the four corners of the cheesecloth and tie them tightly together to maintain the shape of the cabbage while it cooks.

To make the broth, in a large soup pot or stockpot, combine all the ingredients. Add the wrapped cabbage to the pot and bring the broth to a boil over high heat. Reduce the heat to low, cover, and cook until the cabbage and its stuffing are thoroughly heated, 1 to 1¼ hours.

Remove the cabbage from the broth to a bowl and discard the broth. Let the cabbage stand in the cheesecloth for 1 hour before serving. You may also refrigerate the cabbage, its cheesecloth wrap intact, and reheat it the next day for serving.

To reheat, preheat an oven to 350 degrees F. Place the cabbage, still in its cheesecloth wrap, in a dutch oven or other heavy ovenproof dish with a tight-fitting lid, add 1 cup water and cook until the cabbage and stuffing are thoroughly heated, 30 to 40 minutes.

To serve, place the cabbage on a platter or in a shallow bowl. Untie the cheesecloth and slide it out from beneath the cabbage. Serve the cabbage warm, cut into wedges.

CANNELLONI FILLED WITH DANDELION GREENS AND MUSHROOMS

SERVES 4

I FIRST ATE CANNELLONI WHEN I WAS A STUDENT IN AIX-EN-PROVENCE. THREE OR FOUR DOORS DOWN THE STREET FROM WHERE I LIVED ON THE RUE AUDE, JUST OFF THE COURS MIRABEAU, WAS A TINY WORKER'S RESTAURANT MUCH FAVORED BY STUDENTS FOR ITS GOOD FOOD AND CHEAP PRICES. THE TABLES WERE ALL VERY CLOSE TOGETHER, LEAVING JUST ENOUGH ROOM FOR PEOPLE TO SQUEEZE INTO THE CHAIRS. SHEETS OF WHITE PAPER COVERED THE TABLES AND BASKETS OF BREAD AND OPEN UNLA-BELED BOTTLES OF RED WINE WERE SET DOWN ON THE CENTERS. ◉ CANNELLONI, I DISCOVERED, WERE PASTA ROLLS, FILLED AND SAUCED AND THEN TOPPED WITH CHEESE. THEY CAME OUT OF THE RESTAU-RANT'S LITTLE KITCHEN BUBBLING HOT IN INDIVIDUAL RAMEKINS, THE SAUCE AND CHEESE FORMING A SORT OF CRUST. I LEARNED TO DIP MY BREAD INTO THE SAUCE WHILE I WAITED FOR THE CANNELLONI TO COOL. ◉ PACKAGED CANNELLONI SHELLS, WHICH ARE READILY AVAILABLE ALL OVER FRANCE, ARE NOT SO EASY TO COME BY HERE, BUT MANICOTTI SHELLS MAKE A GOOD SUBSTITUTE.

Preheat an oven to 350 degrees F.

In a heavy-bottomed saucepan over medium heat, melt 3 tablespoons of the butter. When it begins to foam, remove the pan from the heat and whisk in the flour, 1 teaspoon of the salt, the black pepper, and cayenne pepper. Return the pan to medium heat and gradually whisk in the 1½ cups milk, adding it in a steady stream. Reduce the heat to low and stir until there are no lumps. Simmer, stirring occasionally, until the sauce becomes thick enough to coat the back of a spoon, about 10 minutes. Remove from the heat and drizzle the surface of the sauce with the 1 tablespoon milk to make a protective film. Set aside.

In a skillet over medium heat, melt 5 tablespoons of the butter. When it begins to foam, add the green onions and sauté until translucent, 3 or 4 minutes. Add the mushrooms and sauté until the color changes slightly, 2 or 3 minutes, but no longer. Stir in the dandelion or other greens and cook until just limp, another minute or two. Stir in the remaining 1 teaspoon salt, and remove from the heat. Stir in ½ cup of the sauce and the bread crumbs to make a paste.

Using a knife, spoon, or your fingers, fill each cannelloni or manicotti shell with some of the paste. Using 1½ tablespoons of the remaining butter, grease 4

11 tablespoons butter

3 tablespoons all-purpose flour

2 teaspoons salt

½ teaspoon freshly ground black pepper

¼ teaspoon cayenne pepper

1½ cups plus 1 tablespoon milk

½ cup minced green onions, including the tender green tops

1 pound fresh mushrooms, such as shiitake, portobello, or cultivated white or brown button, chopped

1 bunch dandelion, chicory, chard, or spinach, or a combination, chopped (2 cups)

¼ cup fine dried bread crumbs

1 cup grated Gruyère cheese

24 *cannelloni shells, each 4 inches long,*
or 12 manicotti shells, precooked
according to package instructions
and cooled

individual ramekins or a single baking dish that will hold the cannelloni snugly. Arrange the filled shells in the prepared dishes or dish. Reheat the sauce over medium-low heat, whisking in the milk covering the top. Add three-fourths of the Gruyère, whisking it in until it melts. Do not overcook. Pour the sauce over the filled shells, blanketing the dishes from edge to edge.

Sprinkle the top(s) with the remaining ¼ cup cheese and dot with the remaining 1½ tablespoons butter. Bake until slightly golden and the sauce is bubbling, 10 to 15 minutes.

Remove from the oven and serve immediately.

LAYERED MOUNTAIN CHEESE, BREAD, AND CABBAGE SOUP

SERVES 4 TO 6

THIS STRONG AND STURDY SOUP IS MADE FROM THE HUMBLEST OF INGREDIENTS, BUT IS WORTHY OF ANY TABLE WHERE SIMPLE LOCAL FOOD IS APPRECIATED. CABBAGE AND ONIONS ARE SIMMERED IN BROTH AND THEN LADLED INTO A DEEP BAKING DISH WITH LAYERS OF DAY-OLD BREAD AND SHARP CHEESE. THE DISH IS BAKED UNTIL THE CHEESE MELTS INTO THE SOUP, THE BREAD ABSORBS THE BROTH, AND THE TOP BECOMES A CRUNCHY GOLDEN CROWN.

2 tablespoons butter

1 small head green cabbage, cored and coarsely chopped

2 yellow onions, chopped

1 teaspoon salt

2 teaspoons freshly ground black pepper

2 juniper berries, crushed

4 cups Basic Vegetable Broth (page 22) or other vegetable broth

6 slices day-old dark, sturdy country-style bread, such as rye or pumpernickel

¼ pound medium-dry cheese, such as Cantal, Edam, or Gruyère, grated

Preheat an oven to 375 degrees F.

In a large skillet over medium heat, melt 1½ tablespoons of the butter. When it begins to foam, add the cabbage and the onions and sprinkle them with the salt, pepper, and juniper berries. Reduce the heat to medium-low, cover, and cook until the cabbage has wilted and reduced in volume, 5 or 6 minutes. Remove the cover, stir the vegetables, re-cover, and continue to cook until thickened and bubbling, another 5 or 6 minutes.

In a large saucepan or soup pot, bring the broth to a boil. Transfer the cabbage and the onions, along with their cooking juices, to the boiling broth. Reduce the heat to medium-low and simmer, uncovered, for 30 minutes.

Drain the cabbage and onions, reserving the broth. Ladle half of the cabbage and onions into a large, deep ovenproof casserole. Arrange 4 of the bread slices on top and then strew with three-fourths of the cheese. Ladle 1½ cups of the reserved broth into the casserole. Add the remaining cabbage and onions in a layer on top and ladle in enough of the remaining broth just to cover the cabbage. Top with the remaining bread slices and cheese and dot with the remaining butter.

Put the dish in the oven and bake until the cheese has melted and the crust is golden, about 15 minutes.

Remove from the oven and scoop into serving bowls.

RATATOUILLE

SERVES 4 TO 6

PERFUMED WITH THE REGION'S OLIVE OIL, WILD THYME, AND GARLIC, **RATATOUILLE** IS THE SUM-MER VEGETABLE STEW OF SOUTHERN FRANCE. FROM JULY THROUGH SEPTEMBER, IT IS EATEN HOT AS A MAIN DISH, COLD AS A FIRST COURSE, AND HOT OR COLD AS AN ACCOMPANIMENT TO PASTAS, OMELETS, AND POLENTA. IT CAN BE SERVED IN INDIVIDUAL RAMEKINS AND TOPPED WITH A FLAKY CRUST, OR USED AS A TOPPING FOR CHEESE-FILLED CRÊPES OR CANNELLONI. ◉ CLASSICALLY, THE DIF-FERENT VEGETABLES ARE COOKED SEPARATELY, THEN COMBINED AT THE END WITH THE TOMATOES. I HAVE NEVER EATEN A **RATATOUILLE** COOKED THAT WAY AT THE HOME OF FRENCH FRIENDS, HOWEVER, ALTHOUGH I HAVE OCCASIONALLY MADE IT THAT WAY MYSELF. INSTEAD, MY FRIENDS INVARIABLY GO INTO THEIR GARDENS; HARVEST THE ABUNDANCE OF ZUCCHINI, SWEET PEPPERS, EGGPLANT, TOMATOES, AND BASIL; RETURN TO THE KITCHEN; AND COOK THE VEGETABLES TOGETHER TO MAKE A SCRUMPTIOUS PLATE. THE PROPORTIONS VARY ACCORDING TO THE HARVEST.

¼ cup olive oil

4 cloves garlic, crushed and minced

2 medium-sized yellow onions, chopped

2 medium-sized eggplants, unpeeled, cut
     into 1-inch cubes

4 medium-sized zucchini, cut into
     1-inch cubes

3 large green, red, or yellow sweet pep-
     pers, seeded, deribbed, and cut into
     1-inch squares

2 tablespoons minced fresh thyme

1 bay leaf

3 ½ to 4 pounds ripe tomatoes
     (10 to 12 medium-sized),
     peeled and chopped

½ teaspoon salt

½ teaspoon freshly ground black pepper

¼ cup minced fresh basil

In a large, heavy-bottomed saucepan or soup pot over medium heat, warm the olive oil. Just as it begins to smoke, reduce the heat to medium-low and add the garlic and onions. Sauté until translucent, 3 to 4 minutes. Add the eggplants, stir well, and sauté for 3 or 4 minutes longer. Then add the zucchini and sweet peppers and continue to sauté, stirring and turning until well coated with oil and slightly softened, another 4 or 5 minutes.

Add the thyme, bay leaf, tomatoes, salt, and black pepper. Stir and turn another 2 or 3 minutes, then cover the pan and reduce the heat to low. Cook, stir-ring occasionally, until the vegetables are soft and have blended together, about 40 minutes.

Stir in the basil and remove from the heat. Transfer to a serving dish and serve hot, at room temperature, or cold.

GNOCCHI WITH GORGONZOLA AND WINTER SAVORY

MAKES ABOUT 60 *GNOCCHI*; SERVES 4

GOOD **GNOCCHI** REQUIRES DRY POTATOES. WHEN MY NEIGHBOR IN FRANCE TAUGHT ME TO MAKE **GNOCCHI**, SHE TOOK ME DOWN INTO HER **CAVE** TO GET THE POTATOES. IT WAS LATE IN THE WINTER, NEARLY SPRING, AND THE SHRIVELED POTATOES REMAINING FROM THE LATE-SUMMER HARVEST WERE ON ONE SMALL CORNER OF THE DIRT FLOOR. SHE EXPLAINED THAT THESE WERE EXCELLENT FOR MAKING **GNOCCHI** BECAUSE DRY POTATOES MAKE THE BEST **PÂTE**. THESE PLUMP POTATO DUMPLINGS, SLIPPERY ON THE OUTSIDE AND FLUFFLY INSIDE, ARE WELL-ADAPTED TO BEING ROLLED AND SLATHERED IN A SALTY, TANGY SAUCE OF GORGONZOLA SPIKED WITH THE DISTINCTIVE WILD-HERB FLAVOR OF WINTER SAVORY. THE TASTES AND TEXTURES MAKE EVERY FORK FULL A BALANCED BITE.

Place the potatoes in a saucepan and add water to cover generously. Bring to a boil and boil until tender, about 30 minutes. Drain well and, when cool enough to handle, peel the potatoes. When the potatoes are cool, using the large holes of a hand-held grater, grate the potatoes into a large bowl. Add the egg and flour and mix well with a fork.

Lightly flour a work surface and turn the potato mixture out onto it. Knead the potato mixture until it is soft and sticky, 4 or 5 minutes.

Bring a large pot filled with water to a boil. While the water is heating, make the *gnocchi*. Take a large handful of the dough and roll it between the palms of your hands to make a rope about 12 inches long and 1 inch in diameter. Cut the rope in half and roll one-half between the palms of your hands to make another 12-inch-long rope, which should now be about ½ inch in diameter. Repeat with the other half.

Cut the ropes into ½-inch-long pieces. Lightly coat the pieces with flour, set them aside, and cover with a damp cloth until you are ready to cook them. Repeat this process until all of the dough has been formed into *gnocchi*. Preheat an oven to 250 degrees F. Place a serving dish large enough to hold all the cooked *gnocchi* in the oven.

When the water is boiling and just before adding the *gnocchi*, add the salt to the pot. Slip the *gnocchi* into the boiling water, 2 or 3 dozen at a time; do not crowd them in the pot. (You can cook the *gnocchi* all at once by using 2 large pots of

2 ½ pounds russet or other baking
  potatoes

1 egg

1 cup all-purpose flour

1 ½ teaspoons salt

1 cup heavy cream

3 ounces Gorgonzola or other creamy
  blue cheese, cut into small pieces

1 teaspoon minced fresh winter savory

water.) Cook the *gnocchi* for 3 or 4 minutes. They are done as soon as they float to the surface. Remove them with a slotted spoon and put them onto the warmed dish, returning it to the oven. Cook the remaining *gnocchi* in the same way.

Meanwhile, prepare the sauce. Heat the cream in a small saucepan over medium heat. Add the cheese, reduce the heat to low, and whisk until the cheese melts. Do not boil. Pour the sauce over the *gnocchi* and sprinkle the winter savory across the top. Serve immediately.

MIXED GRILL OF WINTER VEGETABLES
WITH DRIED-TOMATO AÏOLI

SERVES 4 TO 6

EACH OF THESE VEGETABLES RETAINS ITS DISTINCT FLAVOR AND TEXTURE WHEN GRILLED. THE PUMPKIN IS NUTTY AND DENSELY CREAMY. THE PARSNIPS CARAMELIZE ON THE OUTSIDE, YET RETAIN THEIR SOFT STARCHINESS INSIDE. THE BROCCOLI FLORETS TURN A BIT CRISPY, AND THE THICK ONION SLICES CHAR ON THE SURFACE AND SWEETEN. THE FULL, RICH FLAVOR OF THE **AÏOLI** IMBUED WITH THE COLOR AND ZEST OF THE DRIED TOMATO WEAVES TOGETHER ALL THE FLAVORS. ⊛ THIS GRILLED VEGETABLE PLATTER MIGHT BE PRECEDED BY A SIMPLE MIXED GREEN SALAD OR A MORE ELABORATE FRISÉE SALAD WITH WARM GOAT CHEESE (PAGE 71).

Place the pumpkin slices on a steamer rack over boiling water, cover, and steam until they are almost tender but still offer a bit of resistance when pierced with the tip of a sharp knife, about 15 minutes. Alternatively, immerse the slices in boiling water and parboil for about 15 minutes, then drain. Set aside.

Cut off the narrow tail of the parsnips and discard. Cut the remaining root lengthwise into ½-inch-thick slices. Cut the broccoli stalks lengthwise into 2 or 3 pieces; the number will depend upon the thickness of the stalks. Steam or parboil the parsnips and broccoli in the same manner as you did the pumpkin, but reduce the time to 4 to 5 minutes. Set aside. Cut the onions into generous ¼-inch-thick slices.

In a small bowl, whisk together the olive or walnut oil, garlic, lemon juice, peppercorns, juniper berries, and salt. Add the rosemary. In a large, shallow baking dish, tray, or bowl, layer half of the vegetables. Drizzle with the olive oil mixture and add another layer of vegetables. Turn the vegetables gently until well coated. Let stand at room temperature for several hours.

Prepare a fire in a charcoal or other grill, or preheat a broiler.

Place the vegetable slices on the grill rack or a broiler pan and grill or broil, turning once, until the vegetables are tender when pierced with a fork, about 8 minutes on each side for the pumpkin, parsnips, and onions and slightly less for the broccoli.

Arrange the vegetables on a platter. Serve the *aïoli* in a bowl alongside.

8 peeled pumpkin slices, each about 2
    inches in diameter and ½ inch thick

4 parsnips

4 broccoli stalks

3 large red or yellow onions

½ cup olive or walnut oil

2 cloves garlic, crushed

Juice of 2 lemons

5 whole black peppercorns, cracked

4 juniper berries, crushed

¼ teaspoon salt

4 fresh rosemary sprigs, each
    6 inches long

Dried-Tomato Aïoli *(page 28)*

FETTUCCINE WITH FAVA BEANS AND PARMESAN DENTELLES

MEATY, BRIGHT GREEN FAVA BEANS LEND SUBSTANCE TO THIS SIMPLE PASTA DISH, AS DO THE LACY CURLS OF SHAVED PARMESAN. FRESH ENGLISH PEAS WOULD MAKE A SOMEWHAT LIGHTER PREPARATION, AND FOR FALL OR WINTER, GRILLED RADICCHIO WOULD BE A GOOD SUBSTITUTE.

1 pound fava beans

¾ pound dried fettuccine

3 tablespoons butter

2 tablespoons minced shallots

¼ cup Leek and Mushroom Broth (page 20) or other vegetable broth

1 teaspoon salt

1 teaspoon freshly ground black pepper

2 ounces Parmesan cheese, shaved into paper-thin slices with a knife or vegetable peeler

½ teaspoon minced fresh thyme

Shell the fava beans and discard the pods. Then remove the thin peel that coats each bean by slitting the edge with a knife and "popping" the bean out. You should have about 1 cup beans. Place the favas on a steamer rack over boiling water, cover, and steam until tender and easily pierced with a fork, about 10 minutes.

While the favas are cooking, bring a large pot filled with salted water to a boil. Add the fettuccine and cook until al dente, about 8 minutes or according to the package directions.

At the same time, in a small saucepan over medium heat, melt 2 tablespoons of the butter. When it begins to foam, add the shallots and sauté until translucent, 3 to 4 minutes. Add the broth and ½ teaspoon each of the salt and pepper. Keep warm over low heat until ready to serve.

When the fettuccine is done, drain it and put it in a warmed serving bowl or on a platter. Add the remaining 1 tablespoon butter, the shallot-broth mixture, and the remaining ½ teaspoon each salt and pepper. Toss until well coated. Fold in the fava beans and three-fourths of the Parmesan cheese. Garnish with the remaining Parmesan and the thyme.

Serve immediately.

RAGOUT OF WILD MUSHROOMS

SERVES 3 OR 4

ITASTED THIS DISH SEVERAL YEARS AGO AT A FRIEND'S HOUSE IN SOUTHERN FRANCE. IT WAS THE END OF MUSHROOM SEASON, AND SEVERAL OF US HAD SPENT THE DAY COMBING THE PINE-AND-OAK-COVERED HILLS WITH OUR KNIVES AND BASKETS. THE MAJORITY OF MUSHROOMS WE FOUND WERE **PETITS GRIS,** SMALL GRAY CAPS WITH A DELICATE FLAVOR AND A HIGH WATER CONTENT. WE DISCOVERED THE LAST OF THE SEASON'S MEATY **SANGUINES** AND CHANTERELLES, PLUS A FEW POCKETS OF FIRM, CREAMY WHITE **PIEDS DE MOUTON.** COOKED DOWN TO THEIR ESSENCE AND SERVED WITH CRUSTY COUNTRY FRENCH BREAD, THEY WERE SUBLIME. ◉ THIS RECIPE USES CULTIVATED MUSHROOMS, PLUS CHANTERELLES. I DO NOT UNDER ANY CIRCUMSTANCES ADVISE YOU TO COLLECT WILD MUSHROOMS WITHOUT THE KNOWLEDGEABLE GUIDANCE OF AN EXPERT. SPOON THE RAGOUT OVER BROILED BAGUETTE SLICES OR STEAMED RICE, IF YOU LIKE.

1 pound fresh oyster mushrooms

1 pound assorted fresh mushrooms, such as chanterelle, shiitake, portobello, cultivated white, or hedgehog, in any combination

4 tablespoons butter

2 tablespoons minced shallots

1½ tablespoons all-purpose flour

½ teaspoon salt

⅛ teaspoon freshly ground black pepper

½ cup dry white wine

2 tablespoons minced fresh parsley

Clean the mushrooms carefully, removing any bits of clinging dirt. Cut the large ones, including their stems, into several pieces. Leave the small mushrooms whole or halve them.

In a heavy-bottomed saucepan over medium heat, melt the butter. When it begins to foam, add the shallots and sauté until translucent, 3 or 4 minutes. Reduce the heat to low and add the mushrooms. Cook, turning the mushrooms often, until they begin to release their juices and create the beginning of a broth, 5 to 10 minutes. Raise the heat to medium and sprinkle the flour, salt, and pepper over the mushrooms, then turn them several times to ensure that they are well coated with the flour. Add the wine and stir for 3 or 4 minutes. By now the mushrooms will have reduced in volume by one-half or more, depending upon your mixture, and you will have about 1 cup of thickened broth. Using a slotted spoon, remove the cooked mushrooms to a plate.

Increase the heat to high and reduce the broth to about ¾ cup. Reduce the heat to low and return the mushrooms to the pan, folding them into the thickened broth and reheating them thoroughly.

Transfer to a warmed serving dish, garnish with the parsley, and serve immediately.

FLUFFY BREAD AND YELLOW ZUCCHINI TIAN

SERVES 4

THIS DISH IS LIGHT AND AIRY, REMINISCENT OF A SOUFFLÉ, BUT IT IS MUCH SIMPLER TO MAKE. USE THE SMALLEST YELLOW ZUCCHINI AVAILABLE, AS THE LARGER ONES ARE TOO WATERY AND WILL ALTER THE TEXTURE OF THE DISH. GREEN ZUCCHINI CAN BE USED IF YELLOW ONES ARE UNAVAILABLE. YOUNG CARROTS, CELERY ROOT, OR TURNIPS COULD BE USED IN PLACE OF THE SQUASH, DEPENDING UPON THE SEASON. ROASTED GARLIC AND FRESH GOAT CHEESE ARE GOOD ACCOMPANIMENTS TO THE TIAN, ALONG WITH A SALAD OF WILD GREENS OR CHICORY.

12 to 16 small yellow zucchini (about
   1 pound total weight), each about
   4 inches long

4 to 6 slices day-old bread

2 cups hot water, or to cover

4 tablespoons olive oil

½ yellow onion, minced

2 garlic cloves, minced

1 tablespoon minced fresh tarragon
   or chervil

¼ cup minced fresh parsley

1 teaspoon salt

1 teaspoon freshly ground black pepper

2 ounces Gruyère, Monterey Jack,
   or other mild cheese, grated

1 egg, lightly beaten

Preheat an oven to 350 degrees F.

Slice the zucchini into wafer-thin slices; set aside. Put the bread in a large bowl and pour in the hot water to cover. Let soak until you can easily squeeze the bread into a paste with your hands, about 20 minutes.

While the bread is soaking, heat 3 tablespoons of the olive oil in a skillet over medium heat. Add the onion and garlic and sauté until translucent, 6 to 7 minutes. Raise the heat a little and add the zucchini. Cook quickly, stirring constantly, until the slices are just a little brown, 3 to 4 minutes. Remove from the heat.

Squeeze the bread dry. Put it in a large bowl and pull it apart into tiny pieces. Add the tarragon or chervil, parsley, zucchini and all the juices from the skillet, salt, pepper, grated cheese, and egg. Mix well.

Select a baking dish 1½ to 2 inches deep and large enough to fill almost to the brim with the zucchini mixture. Oil the dish with half of the remaining olive oil. Add the bread-zucchini mixture, smoothing it evenly in the dish. Drizzle the surface with the remaining olive oil. Bake until the surface is crisp and golden and a knife inserted into the center comes out clean, about 30 minutes.

Scoop out with a serving spoon onto warmed individual plates. Serve piping hot.

COUSCOUS WITH SPRING VEGETABLES

SERVES 4 TO 6

COUSCOUS IS A POPULAR NORTH AFRICAN PASTA THAT IS OFTEN SERVED WITH A PIQUANT STEW AND FURTHER SPICED WITH **HARISSA**. COUSCOUS HAS BECOME PART OF THE FRENCH TABLE BECAUSE OF THE FRENCH COLONIZATION OF NORTH AFRICA IN THE NINETEENTH CENTURY, FOLLOWED BY IMMIGRATION FROM THAT REGION TO FRANCE. ◉ COUSCOUS RESTAURANTS THROUGHOUT PARIS AND THE PROVINCES FEATURE SPICY VEGETABLE-ONLY STEWS USING SEASONAL VEGETABLES OF THE REGION.

2 tablespoons butter

2 tablespoons olive oil

2 yellow onions, chopped

2 cloves garlic, chopped

½ teaspoon salt

½ teaspoon freshly ground black pepper

1 teaspoon minced fresh thyme

2 tablespoons ground turmeric

2 small bird's eye or other small dried
*   red chili peppers, seeded and crumbled*

⅛ teaspoon saffron threads

8 small new potatoes, unpeeled,
*   halved crosswise*

1 small head cauliflower, cut into florets
*   with tender stems intact*

8 small carrots

2 cups Leek and Mushroom Broth (page
*   20) or other vegetable broth*

1 cup shelled English peas

10 ounces instant couscous

Harissa *(page 33)*

¼ cup minced fresh mint

¼ cup minced fresh chives

¼ cup minced fresh tarragon

In a deep skillet or dutch oven over medium heat, melt the butter with the olive oil. When they begin to foam, add the onions and garlic and sauté until translucent, 3 or 4 minutes. Stir in the salt, black pepper, thyme, turmeric, chilies, and saffron. Then add the potatoes, cauliflower, and carrots, turning them gently in the butter mixture for a minute or two. Pour the broth over the vegetables and stir for a minute or two. Cover tightly and reduce the heat to low. Cook until the potatoes are almost tender when pierced with the tip of a knife, 15 to 20 minutes.

Add the peas, re-cover, and cook until the peas and potatoes are tender, another 5 to 7 minutes.

About 10 minutes before the vegetables are done, begin preparing the couscous according to the package instructions and prepare the hot sauce. In a small serving bowl, stir together the mint, chives, and tarragon.

Spoon the couscous and vegetable stew into separate serving bowls. Serve the *Harissa* and the herbs alongside for guests to add as desired.

FRESH FAVA BEANS BAKED WITH WHOLE BABY GARLIC

SERVES 3 OR 4

AS THEY COOK, THE FAVAS SOAK UP THE SUBTLE FLAVOR OF THE SMALL, GREEN ONIONLIKE BULBS OF BABY GARLIC AND THE RESINOUS FRESH ROSEMARY. THIS IS TRADITIONALLY A LATE-SPRING DISH, BECAUSE AT THE SAME TIME THAT THE FAVA PODS ARE PLUMP WITH YOUNG, TENDER BEANS, SHOOTS OF THE GARLIC HAVE LENGTHENED, AND THE GARLIC BULBS, DEEP BENEATH THE GROUND, HAVE BEGUN TO SWELL BUT HAVE NOT YET DEVELOPED INTO CLOVES. ALTHOUGH FAVA BEANS, PARTIC-ULARLY YOUNG ONES, CAN BE COOKED AND EATEN WITHOUT REMOVING THEIR SKINS, THE FLAVOR AND TEXTURE OF THE PEELED BEANS ARE SO EXTRAORDINARY, I RECOMMEND THE PEELING. (NOTE: SOME PEOPLE ARE HIGHLY ALLERGIC TO FAVA BEAN SKINS.)

Preheat an oven to 350 degrees F.

Shell the fava beans and discard the pods. Then remove the thin peel that coats each bean by slitting the edge with a knife and "popping" the bean out. You should have about 2 cups beans.

Arrange the garlic bulbs in the bottom of a baking dish with a cover just large enough to hold the beans in a layer 2 to 3 inches deep. Cover them with the fava beans and sprinkle with the 2 tablespoons rosemary, the salt, and pepper. Drizzle 3 tablespoons of the olive oil evenly over the vegetables. Cover, place in the oven, and bake until the garlic is easily pierced with the tip of a knife, about 40 minutes.

Remove from the oven and drizzle with the remaining 1 tablespoon olive oil. Garnish with rosemary and serve hot directly from the dish.

2 to 2 ½ pounds fava beans

8 heads baby garlic, tough outer
    skins removed

2 tablespoons chopped fresh rosemary,
    plus chopped fresh rosemary for
    garnish

½ teaspoon salt

½ teaspoon freshly ground black pepper

4 tablespoons olive oil

GRATIN OF RED AND YELLOW CHERRY TOMATOES WITH RICOTTA AND BASIL TOPPING

SERVES 6 TO 8

THE TOMATOES, BOUND TOGETHER AND SCANTILY COVERED WITH THE CUSTARDY RICOTTA MIXTURE, COME OUT OF THE OVEN PIPING HOT, THEIR PLUMP ROUNDS STILL INTACT AND WAITING FOR THE FORK.

Preheat an oven to 425 degrees F.

Choose a shallow baking dish that is just large enough to hold the tomatoes snugly packed in a single layer. Using 2 tablespoons of the olive oil, grease the bottom and sides of the dish. Add the tomatoes, rolling them around to coat them with the oil.

In a small bowl, combine the bread crumbs, garlic, 5 tablespoons of the basil, ¼ teaspoon of the salt, and the pepper. Sprinkle half of the mixture over the oiled tomatoes.

In a mixing bowl, combine the ricotta, the remaining 3 tablespoons basil and ½ teaspoon salt, the eggs, flour, and cream. Stir until well blended and creamy. Pour this mixture over the crumb-topped tomatoes. Sprinkle with the remaining bread crumb mixture and drizzle with the remaining 1 tablespoon olive oil.

Place in the oven and bake until the cheese is slightly browned and the tomatoes have not yet burst, about 15 minutes. Serve hot or at room temperature, spooned onto individual plates.

3 tablespoons olive oil

2 pounds cherry tomatoes, preferably a mixture of red and yellow

¼ cup fine dried bread crumbs

1 clove garlic, minced

½ cup chopped fresh basil

¾ teaspoon salt

1 tablespoon freshly ground black pepper

1 cup ricotta

2 eggs

2 tablespoons all-purpose flour

¼ cup heavy cream

CHARD AND POTATO TERRINE

SERVES 4 TO 6

THIS TERRINE OF ALTERNATING LAYERS OF CHARD AND THINLY SLICED POTATOES, INTERSPERSED WITH CHEESE AND SEASONINGS, IS EQUALLY GOOD HOT OR AT ROOM TEMPERATURE. THE FLAVORS MAY BE VARIED, DEPENDING UPON WHETHER YOU USE STARCHY BAKING POTATOES OR WAXY BOILING POTATOES AND YOUR CHOICE OF CHEESE. A SIMPLE GREEN SALAD OR A PLATTER OF **CRUDITÉS** WOULD BE A GOOD BEGINNING FOR THIS DISH, OR A FINE ACCOMPANIMENT SERVED ALONGSIDE.

6 medium-sized potatoes, such as russet, White Rose, or Yellow Finn

18 baby chard leaves, or 9 large chard leaves, thick midribs removed

1 clove garlic, bruised

6 ½ tablespoons butter

1 ½ tablespoons salt

½ teaspoon freshly ground black pepper

2 to 3 ounces cheese, such as Cantal, Brie, or Gruyère, cut into small pieces

¼ cup heavy cream

Preheat an oven to 350 degrees F.

Slice the potatoes as thinly as possible. Set them aside. Coarsely chop the chard leaves. Rub a standard loaf pan with the garlic and ½ tablespoon of the butter. Arrange one-third of the potatoes in a layer in the pan. Sprinkle with one-third each of the salt and pepper, dot with 1 ½ tablespoons of the butter, and top with one-third of the chard leaves. Although the chard may seem incredibly bulky, it will wilt during cooking. Sprinkle one-third of the cheese over the chard. Repeat the layers twice in the same way, ending with the cheese.

Dot the surface with the remaining 1 ½ tablespoons butter and pour the cream evenly over the top. Cover with aluminum foil and bake until the potatoes are easily pierced with the tip of a knife, about 1 ¼ hours.

Serve hot or warm, sliced into wedges.

CREAMY BEET AND POTATO GRATIN

SERVES 8

THE ROSY-RED CREAM THAT BUBBLES UP BETWEEN THE DARK RED BEETS MAKES THIS A COLORFUL CENTERPIECE DISH TO SERVE ON A SPECIAL OCCASION. THE BEETS AND THE CHEESE ARE AN UNUSUAL BUT EXTREMELY SATISFYING COMBINATION. IN SUMMER, A GOOD FIRST COURSE TO SERVE WOULD BE SALAD OF FRESH SHELL AND SNAP BEANS WITH WINTER SAVORY (PAGE 66), AND IN SPRING, ARTICHOKES STUFFED WITH FENNEL DUXELLES (PAGE 61).

3 pounds beets, unpeeled

1½ pounds baking or boiling potatoes, unpeeled

4 tablespoons butter

½ cup freshly grated Parmesan cheese

¼ cup grated Gruyère cheese

1 teaspoon salt

1 teaspoon freshly ground black pepper

1 tablespoon minced fresh rosemary

1 cup heavy cream

¾ cup milk

⅓ cup fine dried, bread crumbs, preferably homemade

Preheat an oven to 350 degrees F.

Place the beets on a steamer rack over boiling water, cover, and steam until tender when pierced with a knife, 20 to 30 minutes. Remove from the rack and set aside. Steam the potatoes separately in the same way; they should also be tender in 20 to 30 minutes. (The vegetables can also be cooked separately in boiling water for about the same amount of time.) When the beets and potatoes are cool enough to handle, peel them and cut them into ¼-inch-thick slices, still keeping them separated.

Select a gratin dish just large enough to hold three layers of the sliced vegetables. Grease it with 1 tablespoon of the butter. Arrange half of the beets in the bottom of the dish. Sprinkle with one-third each of the Parmesan and Gruyère cheese, salt, pepper, and rosemary. Dot with 1 tablespoon of the butter. Arrange all of the potatoes in a layer atop the beets. Sprinkle with half of the remaining cheeses, salt, pepper, and rosemary. Dot with 1 tablespoon of the butter. Layer the remaining beet slices on top and sprinkle with the remaining cheese, salt, pepper, and rosemary. In a vessel with a spout, combine the cream and milk and pour the mixture evenly over the top. Strew the bread crumbs over the surface and dot with the remaining 1 tablespoon butter.

Place in the oven and bake until the sauce is bubbling and the topping is golden brown, 30 to 40 minutes. Remove from the oven and serve hot or warm, scooping out portions with a spoon.

CHARD AND PARSLEY QUICHE WITH TWO CHEESES

I LIKE TREATING PARSLEY AS A GREEN VEGETABLE, AND ITS FLAVOR, IN THIS RECIPE, PREDOMINATES OVER THAT OF THE CHARD, PARTICULARLY IF FLAT-LEAF PARSLEY IS USED. COOKED PARSLEY HAS A CRISP, CLEAN TASTE THAT IS REFRESHINGLY DIFFERENT FROM OTHER COOKED GREENS.

Preheat an oven to 475 degrees F.

To make the pastry shell, sift together the flour and salt into a bowl. Cut the butter and margarine into ½-inch chunks and add them to the flour mixture. Using a pastry blender or 2 knives, cut in the butter and margarine until the mixture forms pea-sized balls. Add the ice water, 1 tablespoon at a time. At the same time, turn the dough with a fork and then with your fingertips just enough to dampen it. This method will help to keep the pastry light and flaky. Do not overwork the dough or it will become tough. Gather the dough into a ball, wrap it in aluminum foil or plastic wrap, and refrigerate for 15 minutes. (The chilling will make it easier to roll out.)

On a lightly floured work surface, roll out the dough into a round about 11 ½ inches in diameter and ⅛ inch thick. Drape the pastry round over the rolling pin and carefully transfer it to a 10-inch tart pan. Unfold it from the pin and press it gently into the pan. Trim off the overlap even with the pan rim. Line the tart shell with aluminum foil and then add a layer of pastry weights or dried beans. Place the weighted pastry pan on a baking sheet. Place in the oven and bake until faintly golden, 8 or 9 minutes. Remove from the oven, lift out the weights, remove the aluminum foil, and let cool completely on the baking sheet. Reduce the oven heat to 375 degrees F.

To make the filling, arrange the chard leaves on a steamer rack over gently boiling water, cover, and steam for 5 to 7 minutes. The leaves should retain their pretty green color but be greatly reduced in volume. Remove the chard from the steamer and squeeze the leaves to extract any water. Cut the chard into chiffonade strips by stacking them, rolling them up into a thin cigar shape, and then cutting them crosswise in thin shreds. Set aside.

Steam the parsley leaves in the same manner as you did the chard, but reduce

For the pastry shell:

2 cups all-purpose flour

1 teaspoon salt

½ cup (¼ pound) unsalted butter, chilled

3 tablespoons margarine, chilled

6 tablespoons ice water

For the filling:

6 to 8 medium-sized or 3 or 4 large chard leaves, thick midribs removed

1 bunch flat-leaf parsley, stems removed

1 tablespoon olive oil

1 clove garlic, minced

1 ½ cups heavy cream

½ teaspoon salt

½ teaspoon freshly ground black pepper

3 eggs

⅓ cup cubed Bel Paese or similar mild, soft cheese (½-inch cubes)

¼ cup freshly grated Parmesan cheese

2 teaspoons butter

the cooking time to 3 to 5 minutes. Remove from the steamer and squeeze dry as you did the chard. Mince the parsley. Again squeeze the chard and parsley to remove any excess water. Set aside.

Warm the olive oil in a skillet over low heat. Add the garlic and sauté until just soft, 1 or 2 minutes. Add the chard and parsley, reduce the heat to very low, and cook, turning often, until the greens have absorbed the oil. This will take about 5 minutes. Remove from the heat and set aside.

In a large mixing bowl, combine the cream, salt, pepper, and eggs. Beat lightly, then add the olive oil–infused greens and the cheeses. Leaving the partially cooked shell in place on the baking sheet, fill it as full as possible without spilling over the top. Cut the butter into bits and dot the top of the quiche.

Place in the oven and bake until the filling is puffed and golden and a knife inserted in the center comes out clean, about 30 minutes.

Remove from the oven and serve immediately or let cool to room temperature. Cut into wedges to serve.

ONION AND GREEN OLIVE TARTE TATIN

SERVES 6 TO 8

SWEET CARAMELIZED ONIONS, THEIR FLAVOR HEIGHTENED BY THE SHARP, ACIDIC TASTE OF GREEN OLIVES, MELT INTO THE FLAKY PASTRY CRUST AND ITS TOPPING OF ROQUEFORT CHEESE.

Cut the onions into ¼-inch-thick slices and then cut into bite-sized bits. In a large skillet over medium heat, melt the butter with the olive oil until mixture foams. Add the onions, bay leaves, oregano, sugar, and salt. Turn onions once or twice, then reduce the heat to low. Cover and cook for another 15 to 20 minutes. Increase heat to medium and cook, stirring often, until the onions become golden brown, 8 to 10 minutes. Remove from the heat and set aside. Preheat oven to 350 degrees F.

To make the pastry, sift together the flour and salt into a bowl. Stir in the parsley. Cut 7 tablespoons of the butter and the margarine into ½-inch chunks and add them to the flour mixture. Using a pastry blender or 2 knives, cut in the butter until the mixture forms pea-sized balls. Add the ice water, 1 tablespoon at a time. At the same time turn the dough with a fork just enough to dampen it. Gather the dough and press into a ball. The dough will be on the dry side.

On a lightly floured board, roll out the dough into a round large enough to cover the top of a glass pie dish 10 inches in diameter and 2 inches deep.

Using the remaining ½ tablespoon butter, thoroughly butter the bottom and sides of the pie dish. Remove and discard the bay leaves from the onion mixture and stir in the olives. Put the onion mixture into the prepared pie dish, then top with the Roquefort cheese slices.

Drape the pastry round over the rolling pin and carefully transfer it to the pie dish. Position the pastry on top of the dish and press with your fingers, tucking the crust snugly along the edges of the filling. Trim off any excess pastry.

Place in the oven and bake until the crust is golden and the onion mixture at the bottom of the dish has become a rich brown, about 15 minutes.

To serve, run a knife along the edges of the crust to loosen it. Invert a large, flat plate on top of the tart. Holding them together firmly, flip them so that the tart is on the bottom. Jiggle the tart dish a bit and then lift it off; the tart will fall gently onto the plate. Serve hot or warm, cut into wedges.

10 medium-sized yellow onions (about 5 pounds)

6 tablespoons butter

2 tablespoons olive oil

3 fresh or dried bay leaves

2 tablespoons chopped fresh oregano

1 teaspoon sugar

½ teaspoon salt

For the pastry:

1½ cups all-purpose flour

1 teaspoon salt

¼ cup chopped fresh parsley

7½ tablespoons butter, chilled

3 tablespoons margarine, chilled

6 tablespoons ice water

30 to 40 brine-cured green olives, with or without pits

¼ pound Roquefort cheese, cut into thin slices

DEEP-DISH CASSOULET OF FLAGEOLET BEANS

SERVES 8

FLAGEOLETS, SMALL KIDNEY-SHAPED BEANS THAT ARE PALE GREEN TO WHITE, HAVE A FIRM TEXTURE AND AN INTENSE BEAN FLAVOR THAT BRING THEIR PARTICULAR CHARACTER TO A DISH. THEY HOLD THEIR SHAPE WHEN COOKED, AND EVEN WHEN COMBINED WITH OTHER INGREDIENTS AS THEY ARE HERE, THEY DO NOT LOSE THEIR INTEGRITY. A LUSTY ONION **CONFIT**, A FULL-BODIED TOMATO **COULIS**, AND A CRUSTY TOPPING OF BUTTERED BREAD CRUMBS SPIKED WITH FRESH THYME AND WINTER SAVORY UNIFY THE DISH. ❂ DO BE AWARE THAT DRIED BEANS VARY IN TASTE AND COOKING TIME, DEPENDING UPON HOW LONG AGO THEY WERE HARVESTED.

1 pound (about 2 cups) dried flageolet beans or navy beans

2 ½ quarts water

1 teaspoon salt

1 ½ cups Onion Confit (page 35)

1 cup Tomato Coulis (page 34), or 1 ½ cups chopped, fresh tomatoes

1 teaspoon salt

1 teaspoon freshly ground black pepper

1 tablespoon chopped fresh thyme

1 tablespoon chopped fresh winter savory

½ cup freshly made bread crumbs

4 tablespoons butter, melted

Pick over the beans and discard any misshapen ones as well as any stones or grit. Rinse in cold water. Place the beans in a large saucepan and add the water and salt. Bring to a boil, reduce the heat to low, cover, and simmer until the beans are tender and have no hint of crunch when bitten, about 2 hours. Remove from the heat.

Preheat an oven to 350 degrees F.

Drain the beans, reserving ¾ cup of the cooking liquid. Set the beans and liquid aside.

In a flameproof casserole large enough to hold all the ingredients eventually, heat ¼ cup of the *confit* over medium heat, stirring for a minute or two. Add the *coulis* or chopped tomatoes, salt, pepper, and ½ tablespoon each of the thyme and winter savory. Continue to stir, blending together the *confit* and sauce. Add the reserved bean liquid and continue to stir another minute or two. Remove from the heat and add half of the beans and half of the remaining *confit*. Fold the beans, *confit*, and sauce together with a wooden spoon or spatula, being careful not to mash the beans. Add the remaining beans and *confit* and fold together.

Toss the bread crumbs in the melted butter and add the remaining ½ tablespoon each thyme and winter savory. Sprinkle the top of the beans with the bread crumb mixture.

Place in the oven and bake until the topping has formed a golden crust and the juices are bubbling around the edge, 15 to 20 minutes. Remove from the oven and slip under a preheated broiler for 2 or 3 minutes to brown the top nicely.

Bring hot to the table and serve with a spoon.

VEGETABLE POT AU FEU

SERVES 6 TO 8

ALTHOUGH A **POT AU FEU** TRADITIONALLY INCLUDES MEAT AND VEGETABLES, THE ALLURE FOR ME HAS ALWAYS BEEN THE VEGETABLES. LEEKS, PARSNIPS, AND TURNIPS, ONIONS AND CARROTS — HUMBLE FOODS ALL — BECOME SUBLIME WHEN SIMMERED IN RICH BROTH AND EATEN BITE BY BITE WITH CORNICHONS AND TINY SOUR ONIONS AND A SPREAD OF HOT MUSTARD OR HORSERADISH OR THICK HOMEMADE MAYONNAISE. THE BROTH, INTENSE WITH THE FLAVOR OF THE VEGETABLES, IS USUALLY RESERVED FOR THE NEXT DAY, WHEN IT IS COOKED WITH TINY PASTA TO MAKE A SOUP. ◉ VARIOUS VEGETABLES CAN BE USED IN A **POT AU FEU**, BUT LEEKS AND CARROTS SHOULD ALWAYS BE INCLUDED, AS THEIR NATURAL SUGARS ARE INTEGRAL TO THE FLAVOR OF THE BROTH. TURNIPS AND RUTABAGAS, USED SPARINGLY BECAUSE OF THEIR POWERFUL, STRONG FLAVORS, ARE ALSO ESSENTIAL INGREDIENTS.

In a saucepan or soup pot large enough to hold all the vegetables eventually, combine the broth, water, salt, pepper, and peppercorns. Tie the bay leaves, parsley, and thyme together with kitchen string or twine to make a bouquet garni and add to the pan, along with the carrots, leeks, onions, turnips, potatoes, and parsnips. Bring to a boil over medium heat. Reduce the heat to low, cover, and simmer for 20 minutes.

Add the celery hearts, re-cover, and simmer for another 20 minutes. Then remove the cover and simmer until all the vegetables are tender when pierced with the tip of a knife, but still hold their shape, about 20 minutes longer. Drain the vegetables and reserve the broth for another use.

Arrange the vegetables on a platter and serve with cornichons and tiny onions, mustard or horseradish, and mayonnaise in small bowls alongside. Alternatively, serve the vegetables in bowls with a ladle of broth poured over them.

4 cups Leek and Mushroom Broth (page 20), or other vegetable broth

2 cups water

1½ teaspoons salt

1 teaspoon freshly ground black pepper

8 whole black peppercorns

2 fresh or dried bay leaves

4 fresh parsley sprigs, each 4 inches long

5 fresh thyme sprigs, each 4 inches long

4 carrots, peeled and cut into 2-inch lengths

4 leeks, white part only, cut into 2-inch lengths

3 small yellow onions, peeled

3 small turnips, peeled and halved

3 boiling potatoes, such as Yellow Finn or Red or White Rose, halved

2 parsnips, peeled and cut into 2-inch lengths

2 celery hearts, each 6 inches long

CHAPTER FOUR

FRUIT
DESSERTS

FRUIT DESSERTS

✳

DESSERTS MADE IN FRENCH HOUSEHOLDS TEND TO BE QUITE SIMPLE AND ARE USUALLY MADE WITH SEASONAL FRUITS AND/OR NUTS. More elaborate desserts, such as multilayered cakes, whipped cream pastries, and other time-consuming and delicate preparations, are purchased at one of the *pâtisseries* that are found even in small villages.

A golden-crusted bread pudding oozing with freshly gathered blueberries or sweet local nectarines is every bit as welcome as a chocolate *ganache* torte or *petit four*. Fresh fruit *clafoutis* are so easy to make they are often one of the first dishes children learn to prepare, proudly carrying the browned, puffed custard to the table themselves. Fresh-fruit ice creams, crêpes filled with fruit and topped with whipped cream, and open-faced tarts are also common homemade dessert fare.

WILD STRAWBERRY TARTS

MAKES EIGHT 4-INCH TARTS

WILD STRAWBERRIES CAN STILL BE FOUND NOT ONLY IN FRANCE'S VALLEYS AND WOODS, BUT THEY ARE CULTIVATED BY SPECIALTY GROWERS AS WELL. OFTEN NO LARGER THAN A SMALL GRAPE, THESE DELICATE **FRAISES DES BOIS** HAVE A NECTARLIKE SWEETNESS.

Preheat an oven to 350 degrees F.

To make the tart shells, sift together the flour and salt into a bowl. Cut the butter and margarine into ½-inch chunks and add them to the flour mixture. Using a pastry blender or 2 knives, cut in the butter and margarine until the mixture forms pea-sized balls. Add the ice water, 1 tablespoon at a time. At the same time, turn the dough with a fork and then with your fingertips just enough to dampen it. Do not overwork the dough or it will become tough. Gather the dough into a ball, wrap it in aluminum foil or plastic wrap, and refrigerate for 15 minutes.

On a lightly floured work surface, roll out the dough ⅛ inch thick. Cut out 8 rounds, each 6 inches in diameter. Drape 1 pastry round over the rolling pin and carefully transfer it to a 4-inch tart pan. Unfold it from the pin and press it gently into the pan. Trim off the overlap even with the pan rim. Repeat with the remaining pastry rounds. Line each tart shell with aluminum foil and then add a layer of pastry weights or dried beans.

Place the weighted shells in the preheated oven for 5 to 6 minutes. Remove them from the oven, lift out the weights, and remove the aluminum foil. Prick each shell bottom with the tines of a fork. Return the pastry shells to the oven and bake until crisp and lightly browned, about 10 minutes longer. Remove the tart shells from the oven and let them cool completely.

To prepare the filling, combine the jelly, water, sugar, and ¼ cup of the strawberries in a saucepan. Bring the mixture to a boil, crushing the berries with the back of a fork. Continue to cook, stirring, until the mixture is thick enough to coat the back of a spoon without dripping, about 10 minutes. Remove from the heat and let cool until warm but still liquid and not set.

Using a pastry brush, paint the bottom of each tart shell with some of the warm jelly mixture. Stack the berries in 2 layers in each tart shell, then drizzle each tart with a little of the jelly mixture. Serve the tarts the same day they are made.

For the tart shells:

2 cups all-purpose flour

1 teaspoon salt

½ cup (¼ pound) unsalted butter, chilled

3 tablespoons margarine, chilled

6 tablespoons ice water

For the filling:

⅓ cup red currant jelly

¼ cup water

¼ cup sugar

2 cups fraises des bois or other small, flavorful hulled strawberries

PEACH AND NECTARINE CLAFOUTI

SERVES 6 TO 8

A CLAFOUTI IS A FRUIT-FILLED SHALLOW PUDDING THAT BUBBLES, PUFFS, AND BROWNS AS IT BAKES. IT IS INDIGENOUS TO THE CHERRY-PRODUCING REGION OF CENTRAL FRANCE, THE **LIMOUSIN**, AND IS TRADITIONALLY MADE WITH LOCAL CHERRIES (UNPITTED) AND THEN DUSTED WITH CONFECTIONERS' SUGAR. NOW, HOWEVER, THE DISH HAS BEEN ADAPTED BY THE REST OF FRANCE, AND IS EATEN ALMOST EVERYWHERE DURING LATE SPRING AND EARLY SUMMER WHEN CHERRIES ARE IN SEASON. ◉ CLAFOUTIS, WHICH MAY BE MORE CUSTARD OR CAKELIKE DEPENDING UPON THE RATIO OF FLOUR TO EGGS AND MILK, MAY BE MADE SUCCESSFULLY WITH ALMOST ANY FRUIT. IN SPRING AND EARLY SUMMER, APRICOTS ARE USED; IN HIGH SUMMER, PEACHES AND NECTARINES REPLACE THEM; AND LATER, IN EARLY FALL, PRUNE PLUMS, PEARS, OR FIGS MIGHT STAR.

½ tablespoon butter

1 cup milk

¼ cup heavy cream

¼ cup granulated sugar

3 eggs

1 tablespoon vanilla extract

⅛ teaspoon salt

⅔ cup all-purpose flour, sifted

6 nectarines, halved, pitted, and then
    peeled, if desired

4 peaches, halved, pitted, and then peeled,
    if desired

Confectioners' sugar (optional)

Preheat an oven to 350 degrees F.

Using the butter, grease a shallow baking dish just large enough to hold the halved fruit in a snugly fitting single layer.

In a bowl, combine the milk, cream, granulated sugar, eggs, vanilla, salt, and flour. Beat with an electric mixer until the mixture is foamy, about 5 minutes. Pour a layer of the batter ¼ inch deep into the prepared baking dish. Place the dish in the preheated oven for 2 or 3 minutes to set the layer. Remove the dish from the oven. Set the fruit halves, cut side down, in the batter. Pour the remaining batter evenly over the fruits.

Place in the oven and bake until puffed and brown and a knife inserted into the center comes out clean, 30 to 35 minutes.

Serve the *clafouti* warm from the oven, plain or dusted with confectioners' sugar.

NECTARINE BREAD PUDDING

SERVES 6

ANY JUICY, SEASONAL FRUIT, FROM ORANGES, CHERRIES, AND PLUMS TO PERSIMMONS, CAN BE ADDED TO THIS BASIC BREAD PUDDING RECIPE TO MAKE A QUICK, STRAIGHTFORWARD DESSERT. THE STRUCTURE OF WHATEVER STALE BREAD YOU USE WILL DETERMINE WHETHER THE PUDDING IS LIGHT AND FLUFFY OR DENSE AND CUSTARDLIKE. COUNTRY-STYLE BREAD WITH LOTS OF AIR POCKETS WILL PRODUCE THE FORMER, AND FINE, REGULAR-TEXTURED BREAD, THE LATTER. BOTH ARE EQUALLY GOOD.

Preheat an oven to 350 degrees F.

Using 1 tablespoon of the butter, grease a standard loaf pan or other baking dish. Set aside.

Pour the milk into a bowl, using about 4 cups if you are using a fine-textured bread and 6 cups if you are using a coarser bread. Add the eggs, all but 2 tablespoons of the sugar, and the salt. Arrange one-third of the bread slices in the bottom of the prepared pan. Top with a layer of the nectarines. Pour about one-fourth of the egg-milk mixture over the nectarines. Repeat the layers twice, pushing the bread down as you go and ending with a layer of bread. Dot with the remaining 1 tablespoon butter and sprinkle with the remaining 2 tablespoons sugar. Place in the oven and bake until a knife inserted into the center comes out clean and the top is nicely browned, about 45 minutes.

Remove from the oven and serve hot or warm in bowls.

2 tablespoons butter

4 to 6 cups milk

3 eggs

¾ cup sugar

½ teaspoon salt

10 to 12 slices day-old bread, each about 1 inch thick (if thinner, use 15 to 17 slices)

3 or 4 nectarines, halved, pitted, and then peeled, if desired

CRISPY PEAR GRATIN

SERVES 6 TO 8

FRUIT GRATINS ARE COUNTRY-STYLE DESSERTS REPLETE WITH LOCAL FLAVORS. THE LATE-SEASON FRUITS, WHICH TEND TO BE THOSE THAT ARE FIRM AND THUS SUITABLE FOR STORING THROUGH WINTER, HOLD THEIR SHAPES BETTER THAN THE SOFTER SUMMER FRUITS, SUCH AS THE SMOOTH-TEXTURED FRENCH BUTTER PEAR. EITHER WILL PRODUCE A DELECTABLE DESSERT, HOWEVER. THE SCANT AMOUNT OF BATTER IS JUST ENOUGH TO BIND THE CONFECTION TOGETHER, AND THE CRUMBLED SUGAR, BUTTER, AND ALMOND TOPPING MAKES A THIN CRUST OVER THE PEARS. ● FRENCH PRUNE PLUMS, GOLDEN DELICIOUS APPLES, BLUEBERRIES, AND QUINCES (THAT HAVE FIRST BEEN POACHED IN SUGAR SYRUP) ARE ALSO GOOD CHOICES FOR FRUIT GRATINS.

5 tablespoons butter

6 tablespoons sugar

4 small butter, Bosc, or other firm,
    flavorful pears, halved, cored,
    and peeled

1 egg

¼ cup milk

¼ cup all-purpose flour

⅛ teaspoon salt

¼ cup crushed almonds

½ teaspoon dried lavender flowers
    (optional)

1 cup half-and-half or heavy cream

Preheat an oven to 425 degrees F.

Using 2 tablespoons of the butter, heavily butter a 9-inch pie plate, preferably glass. Sprinkle 2 tablespoons of the sugar over the bottom. Place the halved pears cut side down in the pie plate.

In a bowl, beat together the egg, milk, flour, and salt to form a batter. Pour the batter evenly over the pears. In a small bowl, stir together the remaining 4 tablespoons sugar, the almonds, and the lavender, if using. Sprinkle the mixture evenly over the pears. Dot the surface with the remaining 3 tablespoons butter.

Place in the oven and bake until the pears are firm and juicy and are crisping on top, about 15 minutes. Remove from the oven and serve hot or warm by scooping up the pear halves and custard onto individual plates. Pour about 2 tablespoons of the half-and-half or heavy cream over each pear half.

COMPOTE OF ORANGES WITH CRÈME DE CASSIS

SERVES 4

THIS COMPOTE DERIVES ITS INTENSE FLAVOR FROM ORANGE ZEST AND CRÈME DE CASSIS–FLAVORED SYRUP, WHICH IS POURED WHILE STILL HOT OVER THE FRUITS. THE COMPOTE IS ESPECIALLY GOOD WHEN ALLOWED TO STAND A DAY BEFORE SERVING TO ALLOW THE FLAVORS TO BLEND FULLY. IT IS WELL PAIRED WITH SPICY GINGERBREAD OR RICH POUND CAKE, BUT IS ALSO SATISFYING EATEN ON ITS OWN OR WITH A BISCOTTI OR OTHER COOKIE TO DIP IN THE SYRUP.

4 oranges

1 cup water

1 cup sugar

2 whole cloves

½ cup crème de cassis

Using a sharp knife or zester, remove the zest, or orange-colored skin, from 3 of the oranges and set the oranges and zest aside separately. Peel the remaining pith from the 3 oranges, and then remove the peel and any pith from the remaining orange and discard. Cut the 4 oranges into slices a generous ¼ inch thick, remove any seeds, and arrange the orange slices in layers in a shallow bowl.

In a heavy-bottomed saucepan over medium heat, combine the water and sugar. Heat, stirring often, until the sugar dissolves. Add three-fourths of the orange zest (reserve the remaining zest for garnish) and the cloves, reduce the heat to low, and simmer, uncovered, until a thin syrup has formed and the flavors have blended, about 1 hour.

Strain the syrup and discard the zest and the cloves. Stir in the crème de cassis and pour the hot syrup over the oranges. Cover and let stand at room temperature for at least 1 hour before serving. If not serving immediately, refrigerate until ready to serve.

Cut the reserved zest into julienne and garnish the oranges just before serving.

LAVENDER ICE CREAM

MAKES ABOUT 1 QUART; SERVES 6

LAVENDER IS USED WITH **HERBES DE PROVENCE** IN SAVORY DISHES, BUT IT IS ALSO USED TO FLAVOR SWEETS. HERE, THE CUSTARD BASE OF THE ICE CREAM IS INFUSED WITH LAVENDER BLOSSOMS, WITH THE RESULT A SUBTLE, HAUNTING TASTE. ALTHOUGH THIS IS NOT A FRUIT DESSERT, IT IS A CLOSE KIN. THE SAME ICE CREAM BASE CAN BE USED FOR FRUIT ICE CREAM BY OMITTING THE LAVENDER AND ADDING 3 CUPS FRUIT TO THE COOLED MIXTURE. APRICOT OR FIG IS ESPECIALLY DELECTABLE.

3 pesticide-free fresh lavender sprigs, or
   1 tablespoon dried lavender blossoms
3 cups heavy cream
1 cup milk
¾ cup sugar
1 tablespoon vanilla extract
4 egg yolks

Place the fresh or dried lavender on a square of cheesecloth, bring the corners together, and tie with kitchen string. Set aside.

In a large, heavy-bottomed saucepan over medium heat, combine the cream, milk, sugar, and vanilla. Heat, stirring, until the sugar dissolves and the mixture thickens, 6 or 7 minutes.

In a bowl, whisk the egg yolks together until lemon-yellow. Slowly whisk in about 1 cup of the hot cream mixture. When it is well blended, slowly pour the yolk-cream mixture into the hot cream mixture in the saucepan, whisking continuously. Continue to whisk over medium heat as the mixture thickens. When it is thick enough to coat the back of a spoon, after about 10 minutes, remove it from the heat and add the lavender. Let stand until cool.

Once the mixture has cooled, remove and discard the cheesecloth bag. Pour into an ice cream maker and freeze according to the manufacturer's instructions.

INDEX

TABLE OF EQUIVALENTS

THE EXACT EQUIVALENTS IN THE FOLLOWING TABLES HAVE

BEEN ROUNDED FOR CONVENIENCE.

US/UK

oz=ounce
lb=pound
in=inch
ft=foot
tbl=tablespoon
fl oz=fluid ounce
qt=quart

METRIC

g=gram
kg=kilogram
mm=millimeter
cm=centimeter
ml=milliliter
l=liter

WEIGHTS

US/UK	Metric
1 oz	30 g
2 oz	60 g
3 oz	90 g
4 oz (¼ lb)	125 g
5 oz (⅓ lb)	155 g
6 oz	185 g
7 oz	220 g
8 oz (½ lb)	250 g
10 oz	315 g
12 oz (¾ lb)	375 g
14 oz	440 g
16 oz (1 lb)	500 g
1½ lb	750 g
2 lb	1 kg
3 lb	1.5 kg

OVEN TEMPERATURES

Fahrenheit	Celsius	Gas
250	20	½
275	140	1
300	150	2
325	160	3
350	180	4
375	190	5
400	200	6
425	220	7
450	230	8
475	240	9
500	260	10

LIQUIDS

US	Metric	UK
2 tbl	30 ml	1 fl oz
¼ cup	60 ml	2 fl oz
⅓ cup	80 ml	3 fl oz
½ cup	125 ml	4 fl oz
⅔ cup	160 ml	5 fl oz
¾ cup	180 ml	6 fl oz
1 cup	250 ml	8 fl oz
1½ cups	75 ml	12 fl oz
2 cups	500 ml	16 fl oz
4 cups/1 qt	1 l	32 fl oz

LENGTH MEASURES

⅛ in	3 mm
¼ in	6 mm
½ in	12 mm
1 in	2.5 cm
2 in	5 cm
3 in	7.5 cm
4 in	10 cm
5 in	13 cm
6 in	15 cm
7 in	18 cm
8 in	20 cm
9 in	23 cm
10 in	25 cm
11 in	28 cm
12/1 ft	30 cm

All-purpose (plain) flour/ dried bread crumbs/chopped nuts

¼ cup	1 oz	30 g
⅓ cup	1½ oz	45 g
½ cup	2 oz	60 g
¾ cup	3 oz	90 g
1 cup	4 oz	125 g
1½ cups	6 oz	185 g
2 cups	8 oz	250 g

Whole-Wheat (Wholemeal) Flour

3 tbl	1 oz	30 g
½ cup	2 oz	60 g
⅔ cup	3 oz	90 g
1 cup	4 oz	125 g
1¼ cups	5 oz	155 g
1⅔ cups	7 oz	210 g
1¾ cups	8 oz	250 g

Brown Sugar

¼ cup	1½ oz	45 g
½ cup	3 oz	90 g
¾ cup	4 oz	125 g
1 cup	5½ oz	170 g
1½ cups	8 oz	250 g
2 cups	10 oz	315 g

White Sugar

¼ cup	2 oz	60 g
⅓ cup	3 oz	90 g
½ cup	4 oz	125 g
¾ cup	6 oz	185 g
1 cup	8 oz	250 g
1½ cups	12 oz	375 g
2 cups	1 lb	500 g

Raisins/Currants/Semolina

¼ cup	1 oz	30 g
⅓ cup	2 oz	60 g
½ cup	3 oz	90 g
¾ cup	4 oz	125 g
1 cup	5 oz	155 g

Long-Grain Rice/Cornmeal

⅓ cup	2 oz	60 g
½ cup	2½ oz	75 g
¾ cup	4 oz	125 g
1 cup	5 oz	155 g
1½ cups	8 oz	250 g

Dried Beans

¼ cup	1½ oz	45 g
⅓ cup	2 oz	60 g
½ cup	3 oz	90 g
¾ cup	5 oz	155 g
1 cup	6 oz	185 g
1¼ cups	8 oz	250 g
1½ cups	12 oz	375 g

Rolled Oats

⅓ cup	1 oz	30 g
⅔ cup	2 oz	60 g
1 cup	3 oz	90 g
1½ cups	4 oz	125 g
2 cups	5 oz	155 g

Jam/Honey

2 tbl	2 oz	60 g
¼ cup	3 oz	90 g
½ cup	5 oz	155 g
¾ cup	8 oz	250 g
1 cup	11 oz	345 g

Grated Parmesan/Romano Cheese

¼ cup	1 oz	30 g
½ cup	2 oz	60 g
¾ cup	3 oz	90 g
1 cup	4 oz	125 g
1⅓ cups	5 oz	155 g
2 cups	7 oz	220 g